Inspire.

DEVOTIONS FOR BUSY YOUNG PEOPLE

PAUL MARTIN

Inspire – Devotions for busy young people Psalm 37 ©2023 Paul Martin

www.inspiredevotions.com

Psalm 34 - A recipe for faith.
Psalm 139 – Finding identity.
Revelation – Unlocking Revelation
Illustrations by Paul Martin.

Books for Youth Workers:
Inspire. A resource for busy youth workers. Volumes 1, 2 & 3.

Artwork for lightbulb from an original line drawing by Amy Walters. Permission is granted solely for use by Paul Martin in his Inspire series and may not be replicated elsewhere. https://www.bloom-creative.co.uk

To all you busy youngsters out there.
May you receive all of the good things
that God has in store for you!

Be inspired!

ACKNOWLEDGEMENTS

I would like to thank my wonderful wife Deb, my bestest friend in the world. You are a wonderful woman of God, one in a trillion and I'm sooooo thankful for you!

Thank you to Alfie and Henry being patient with me when I'm doing book stuff. You are both growing up to be fine young men. Yous are awesome.

Thank you to Mum and Dad for your prayers and support over the years with everything. Your listening ears and wise words have kept me going through the difficulties! Thank you for checking through the book with oxos to help me find the bits that need altering.

Thank you to Amy Walters for your light bulb line drawing, which has become a logo for my Inspire books. I love the prophetic insight that comes through your art and design work. You are truly gifted.

...and thank you for buying this devotional! I wrote it so that you will find strength and freedom in Jesus to live your life to the full, as you depend on God for so much!

ABOUT THIS BOOK

I wrote this book to help you and encourage you in your life of faith; because let's face it, life has its fair share of challenges. Maybe you don't know God personally, or feel that He's a million miles away. Perhaps you've had some unsettling circumstances that have confused you, or given you more questions than answers. It could be that life has just felt like you're having one battle after another, under the pressure of bullying behaviour. If you're looking for a solution, Psalm 37 will point you in the right direction.

The answers are found by gaining wisdom. Not just any wisdom, but God's wisdom. His wisdom brings His all-knowing perspective on what you're going through. God's wisdom is like a winning lottery ticket ready to be cashed; a priceless masterpiece forgotten about, hidden away in a loft, waiting to be discovered. Wisdom is a priceless thing, because when you put God's wise words into practice, you're in line for a wealth of blessings that money can't buy. The joy of living life or having freedom from worry doesn't seem like that big a deal, until you are unhappy or anxious; then most people will do anything to find the solution to these problems.

This book is called *Making it through*. It's a study of the wise words found in Psalm 37. The wisest thing a person can do is to enjoy friendship with God and take heed of His words. Time with Jesus is time well spent. Yet sometimes, like that missing ticket or forgotten masterpiece, if we don't value God's wise ways or consider deeply His wise words, we'll miss out. So we'll go through the Psalm slowly, verse by verse helping you to understand each part as you draw on the wisdom from God's heart. It's likely you'll feel challenged as you read some of these words. As a teenager, Psalm 37 impacted me powerfully and led me to know God in a much deeper way. Give God every opportunity to work in your life. He wants to change you for good, making you strong to face the challenges ahead.

We all need a bit of wise advice to keep us on track in life and help us through those tricky times. God has something very remarkable that He wants to bring about in your life, as you put His words into practice.

PRAYER SPACE

In this book are pages called "Prayer spaces." I've designed these to help you to connect with God. So there's lots of blank space for you to write or draw as you talk with God. I find that when good thoughts come to mind as I pray, they are often God thoughts. These will be moments where God is speaking to you. Having them recorded on a page enables you to remember God's encouraging words. It's worth re-reading these words to help you stay encouraged, as we can so easily forget them in the busyness of life. The prayer spaces are also there to inspire you. Sometimes when we pray, it can be difficult to know where to start. They can help to lead you to express what is on your heart to God.

It's worth reading a devotion and then taking time to pray. Prayer is best done whilst we're taking in God's words, as the Holy Spirit will use these words to talk to you. You'll also notice "Journal Spaces" too. These are just for you to write down where you are at in life, in your journey with God. A bit like a diary where you can record your thoughts sparked by what you have read. This book is all about being inspired by God's word so that you can live out a life of faith in Jesus, in your busy every day.

May you find wisdom like that lottery ticket and may God speak to you powerfully through the words of this book and may He work new things in your life that encourage you and strengthen you for today and tomorrow! I'm praying for you!

MAKING IT THROUGH

Contents

Contents

PSALM 37

¹ Do not fret because of those who are evil
or be envious of those who do wrong;
² for like the grass they will soon wither,
like green plants they will soon die away.

³ Trust in the LORD and do good;
dwell in the land and enjoy safe pasture.
⁴ Take delight in the LORD,
and He will give you the desires of your heart.

⁵ Commit your way to the LORD;
trust in Him and he will do this:
⁶ He will make your righteous reward shine like the dawn,
your vindication like the noonday sun.

⁷ Be still before the LORD
and wait patiently for Him;
do not fret when people succeed in their ways,
when they carry out their wicked schemes.

⁸ Refrain from anger and turn from wrath;
do not fret—it leads only to evil.
⁹ For those who are evil will be destroyed,
but those who hope in the LORD will inherit the land.

¹⁰ A little while, and the wicked will be no more;
though you look for them, they will not be found.
¹¹ But the meek will inherit the land
and enjoy peace and prosperity.
¹² The wicked plot against the righteous
and gnash their teeth at them;
¹³ but the Lord laughs at the wicked,
for he knows their day is coming.

¹⁴ The wicked draw the sword
and bend the bow
to bring down the poor and needy,
to slay those whose ways are upright.
¹⁵ But their swords will pierce their own hearts,
and their bows will be broken.

¹⁶ Better the little that the righteous have
than the wealth of many wicked;
¹⁷ for the power of the wicked will be broken,
but the LORD upholds the righteous.

¹⁸ The blameless spend their days under the LORD's care,
and their inheritance will endure forever.
¹⁹ In times of disaster they will not wither;
in days of famine they will enjoy plenty.
²⁰ But the wicked will perish:
Though the LORD's enemies are like the flowers of the field,
they will be consumed, they will go up in smoke.

²¹ The wicked borrow and do not repay,
but the righteous give generously;
²² those the LORD blesses will inherit the land,
but those he curses will be destroyed.
²³ The LORD makes firm the steps
of the one who delights in him;
²⁴ though he may stumble, he will not fall,
for the LORD upholds him with his hand.

²⁵ I was young and now I am old,
yet I have never seen the righteous forsaken
or their children begging bread.
²⁶ They are always generous and lend freely;
their children will be a blessing.

²⁷ Turn from evil and do good;
then you will dwell in the land forever.
²⁸ For the LORD loves the just
and will not forsake his faithful ones.
Wrongdoers will be completely destroyed;
the offspring of the wicked will perish.

^{29} The righteous will inherit the land
and dwell in it forever.
^{30} The mouths of the righteous utter wisdom,
and their tongues speak what is just.
^{31} The law of their God is in their hearts;
their feet do not slip.

^{32} The wicked lie in wait for the righteous,
intent on putting them to death;
^{33} but the LORD will not leave them in the power of the wicked
or let them be condemned when brought to trial.

^{34} Hope in the LORD and keep his way.
He will exalt you to inherit the land;
when the wicked are destroyed, you will see it.

^{35} I have seen a wicked and ruthless man
flourishing like a luxuriant native tree,
^{36} but he soon passed away and was no more;
though I looked for him, he could not be found.

^{37} Consider the blameless, observe the upright;
a future awaits those who seek peace.
^{38} But all sinners will be destroyed;
there will be no future for the wicked.

^{39} The salvation of the righteous comes from the LORD;
he is their stronghold in time of trouble.
^{40} The LORD helps them and delivers them;
he delivers them from the wicked and saves them,
because they take refuge in him.

STRESSING OUT
Day 01

Do not fret because of those who do evil,
or be envious of those who do wrong

In England queueing can be a bit of a big deal. I suppose it goes along with the British sense of fair play. It's not written anywhere, like a rule of how to do it; but you just know that if you are there in before everyone else, you deserve to be served next. If not, then you wait your turn.

So I'm in a sandwich shop, admittedly in a world of my own, but as far as could be said I was adhering strictly to the unwritten rules of queueing. I believe the thought taking up most of my brain space was "remember it's BMT not BLT;" when I was interrupted by a young guy talking at me in an aggressive manner. "Excuse me!!" he said angrily, "Don't you know there's other people in this queue?? You have just pushed in!!" All of this was news to me, as I was sure I had joined the back of the queue. Actually, I have never pushed in front in a queue (apart from once in a Sardinian bus station where the queuing system was clearly every man for himself). I couldn't understand it.

Well, this guy was obviously upset and I apologised and went in behind him, feeling really bad.

As I fell in behind the man, the lady behind me said, "Don't worry, you were definitely here before us." It was at this point I began to process what had just gone on and I realised I couldn't have been behind one and in front of the other. This man had just intimidated me into thinking I'd pushed in, giving him the opportunity to queue jump. What an outrage!

Yes. I know what you are thinking... this is hardly the crime of the century! Of course, there are a lot of other worse things I could be talking about, but what I want to show you here is the act of intimidation. Bullies use this all the time, where they try to pressurise and dominate others in order to control them. I'm sure you know of people who use these tactics.

" There's a reason why God says *"Do not fret."* It all has to do with what God is going to do next. "

How do you respond when evil gets its way? When cheaters win, bullies intimidate and people get rich through the misfortune of others? You know, real life situations, where those who succeed do so by using evil to get what they want. It can be stressful and overwhelming when we feel powerless to do anything about it. We want justice, but if we stand up to these people, the worry is that we won't succeed against them. Some have decided that the only way to succeed is to use the same methods. Not so with God. He has an altogether different plan.

I love the first three words of this Psalm, *"Do not fret."* The word fret carries the idea of getting hot with stress and worry. Maybe you've experienced the feeling of deep concern, where you're in conflict with someone who has wronged you, but you feel you're up against unfair odds. Concern about what a bully might do or say next and how to respond can get us stressed out. Maybe the only way is to be like them? No. There's a reason why God says *"Do not fret."* It all has to do with what God is going to do next.

Evil wants its own way, but when it comes into conflict with God's way of doing things, evil doesn't stand a chance. God's starting point in dealing with evil begins by freeing ourselves from the doubt and worry that will try and eat away at our faith. We know that God is the King upon the throne and that there is none greater than Him. This is what prayer is all about. When we cry out to God the Almighty and ask for His help in the battles we are facing, they then become His battles. The enemy does not stand a chance!

PRAY

Father God. Thank You that You want me to invite You into my troubles, to partner with You so that we can navigate through this difficulty together. Thank You that Your way of doing things brings freedom to those who are oppressed. I love Your ways Lord!

Day 01

JOURNAL SPACE

do not fret
BECAUSE
of those
WHO DO EVIL,
or be envious
OF THOSE WHO
do wrong

FADING INFLUENCE
Day 02

*Do not fret because of those who do evil, or be envious
of those who do wrong, for like the grass they will soon
wither, like green plants they will soon die away.*

Fame and influence can be a lot like those crazes that captures every kid's imagination. You know the kind of thing, where a new product is released and all of your mates can't get enough of it and the shops run out of stock. In the 1970s, hula hoops and roller skates were the big thing. During my school days, special edition Coca-Cola Yo-Yos were massively popular. I remember going in to school one day and everyone was doing trick shots like rock the baby and walk the dog. The people at Coca-Cola also produced a rare gold one that was probably worth its weight in real gold!

Tamagotchis, loom bands and fidget spinners; they came into our lives and suddenly everybody wanted them. Each one was the next big thing. Yet within a short period of time their novelty had worn off and they had disappeared from popularity. Before long these things ended up in the back of a wardrobe somewhere, forgotten and disregarded.

The words *"Don't fret,"* talk to our concerns about those evil people who rise to a place of popularity. It can be worrying when people who do evil seem to get their own way. Our fears tempt us to believe they will always hold that place of influence or that we're powerless in comparison. Out of nowhere they establish a platform, a power base, recognised by others as the school bully or the new person in charge, that everyone is in awe of. Yet much like the crazes we've talked about, the popularity and influence for those who do evil is only temporary. Their deeds do not go unnoticed by God. They will fade like a fragile flower, since their roots are not in the Almighty.

Therefore, fretting about those who do evil is a waste of time, their moment in the limelight will be fleeting. Stressing uses up a lot of mental and emotional energy. Is the only way to stop stressing about this stuff to just ignore it? Not quite. Being encouraged to *"not fret"* doesn't mean we turn a blind eye to the injustices that take place, or do nothing to stand against them. God wants you and me to not get stressed into thinking that evil has more power over our lives than it actually does. It's a short-term success, a fake power, a fading influence that has no deep roots to make it last.

" Stressing uses up a lot of mental and emotional energy. "

A step in the right direction is to begin seeing things as God sees them. In the verses of Psalm 37 we're given God's wisdom, from one who has seen life, looking back over the span of their years. Being mindful of God's working over this time, he reflects that God is both loving and full of justice. God may well give a bully the opportunity of a second chance, to turn from their ways. God doesn't want evil to prosper and although these people appear to have the freedom to do evil, it is not a freedom that will last. Criminals will get caught and celebrities will soon be forgotten like yesterday's news when they reject the loving kindness of God.

What can we do to stand strong in such situations? As you read on, you'll discover a way that gains wisdom, courage and faith when we put our roots down in God... but more about that tomorrow!

I want to share God's heart for your heart today. He wants you to lay aside any rage and stress you are currently carrying by releasing it all to God. In return God wants to give you His peace. It's a peace that will give you the confidence to see that good things are waiting for you tomorrow.

PRAY

Father God, as I spend a while with You now, I release to You all the pressures and distractions that might draw me away from this moment with You. I want to know Your peace deep in my heart regarding the challenges from people that I face. In Jesus' name.

Day 02

WAIT AND ASK GOD
TO COME CLOSE

PRAY WITH
AN OPEN BIBLE

MAKE A DISCOVERY
ABOUT WHO GOD IS

ASK FOR HELP

WHAT IS GOD SAYING TO ME THAT I NEED TO DO?

TALK TO GOD ABOUT
WHAT YOU DISCOVER
SHARE YOUR HEART

SHARE YOUR REGRETS

FINDING SECURITY
Day 03

Trust in the LORD and do good; dwell in the land
and enjoy safe pasture.

Have you ever had that moment when you're walking down the street and for a split second you think, "Oh!! Where's my phone??" Your heart stops as you frantically check for it. Then you discover it, there it is, in your bag or your pocket and that feeling of relief seems to restart your heart!

These days our smartphones have become such a handy tool for living that to leave it behind could mess up everything. A while ago, I was on a bus to the airport, but had forgotten which terminal to go to. Time was tight and to get off at the wrong stop would've meant having to wait for another bus and possibly missing the flight. Thankfully I had my phone, so I Googled my flight number, which told me the terminal. Problem solved!

It's a scary thing to ask, "What would I do without my phone??" We're lost without them when they run out of charge! Could we get by without them? Often having a phone with us makes us feel secure. It keeps us connected to our friends, will guide us through unknown places and has all the info ready for helpful sites that we need. These and other useful features give us the feeling of security, that we have all we need. It's like a confidence, making us feel prepared for whatever we might face.

We read the words *"Trust in the Lord and do good; dwell in the land and enjoy safe pasture."* Trusting has to do with placing our confidence in something or someone. We rely on them so much, that if they were to let us down, we would be stuck. Much like the way we treat our phones, God wants us to feel secure in the fact that He is with us; but more than that, He wants us to rely on Him in the times when we need extra help.

When we feel overwhelmed or when evil people get their way, it can make us doubt whether we'll avoid the harm that is threatening to come in our direction. However, God wants us to see things from His perspective. He sees from the beginning of our situation, right through to the end. He says that evil has an influence that is fading, they'll be forgotten in no time. God wants us to see what He sees.

How can we see things God's way? The words *"dwell in the land and enjoy safe pasture,"* give us a step in the right direction. A dwelling is an old word for a place to live. Have you ever been upset by something, only to be told "Don't dwell on it"? God wants us to turn our attention from those negative things and instead to live with our focus on how He the Almighty is with us. Maybe you'd ask, "But what good would that do?" Seeing God as the answer to your difficulties opens the door of faith. God responds to faith by answering and providing what we need. He promises us *"safe pasture"* like a shepherd who finds a safe place for his sheep and stays as a guard over them. When we trust God, we enter His place of safety and will enjoy His help when we need it.

> **"** The words *"dwell in the land and enjoy safe pasture,"* give us a step in the right direction. **"**

If we can put our confidence in God for our daily needs with the level of reliance that we have on our phones, we will see powerful things happen. I simply say to God, "Father God, please fill in the gaps for the things that I can't do." It's not a magic formula, but it's my way of telling God that I am relying on Him for the things that stress me out. I expect you have those days where you wonder how you will get through? We can needlessly fret about things beyond our power to fulfil. This is where God says, "Let me handle that, I'm always working on your behalf. I'll take care of it for you."

PRAY

Father God. Thank You that I can find my security in You. You are a good, good Father. I choose to trust You. I am confident that You are with me, You go ahead of me and are working out answers to things I haven't even asked for yet. I invite You to be King of my life, I'll talk to You throughout my day and enjoy your presence with me. In Jesus' name!

Day 03

TAKING DELIGHT
Day 04

*Take delight in the L*ORD*, and He will give you
the desires of your heart.*

What are some of the things that you really love doing? A Saturday night in, with pizza and a movie? Online gaming with your friends? Could it be meeting up with some friends in town? Or down the park with a football? I almost feel like bursting into song "These are a few of my favourite things!" Each of us has at least one thing we enjoy doing above everything else. Those of us who are particularly creative might really love to find somewhere quiet to read a book, paint on canvas, to write, or play a musical instrument. It's in these moments, we can just get lost in what we're doing, as the hours go by like minutes.

The words we read today tell us that there is great joy and pleasure to be discovered in connecting with God; *"Take delight in the Lord, and He will give you the desires of your heart."* If you think of it, delighting is the opposite of fretting. Rather than getting stressed, it's an enjoyable encounter that thrills the heart. This is what God wants for you to experience on a regular basis. Is it your heart's desire to discover what God is really like? To know Him with your heart, rather than to only imagine what He's like? Here we have a promise from God to you today, that if you genuinely desire to be close to God taking the time to know Him, He will lead you to discover more of Him in a supernatural way.

Think of this for a moment. The God of heaven who created you and me wants us to know Him. This is His invitation to us. He is real and wants us to experience His reality. He made prayer to be an encounter with Him, not a list of things you're supposed to say. Talking to God isn't some mindless chore to do, like brushing your teeth.

"Delighting is the opposite of fretting."

Delighting in God is coming to God with the expectation that He is going to reveal something fresh about Himself to you. It's making a real connection with our Creator, heart to heart. So you can be creative in how you meet with Him. Are you tired? Just lay on the floor in silence and invite God into your space. Maybe you're a lively person and want to play some worship music and jump around? If it's done as a pure offering of yourself to God, where He is the focus, it's prayer and can lead to delighting in Him. Why not open up a beautiful Bible verse and begin to think deeply about what it tells you about God? Then tell Him what you like about what you've discovered! Ask God to come close. God is Spirit; because He is Spirit, He enables you to communicate with Him in many different ways. You can write to Him and like an email, He will see it immediately. You can ask Him to speak to you in picture language and then draw something devoted to Him. Come to God with an expectation that He is in the room and wants to meet with you in a meaningful way. I tell you, like those favourite things that you love to do, you'll always want more time!

God wants you to have a gift that will delight your heart even more than you do! He offers Himself as a real gift for you to discover. Praying can be a bit like an Easter egg hunt. At times it will be easy to find joy as you connect with God. Other times the search will take some effort to break through. There will be days when you feel you aren't discovering God immediately, but if you experience this, don't give up, you will find Him. Above all else, expect God to be there with you. He has given you this gift of an encounter with Him. He wants to share this time with you. Go by the clock if necessary. Maybe for a week intend to pray for five minutes each day; then the following week make it eight minutes. Before long, you'll want more and more time with God, because you'll find you're really connecting with Him. Always read something from the Bible that tells you more about Him. See what unfolds in your mind as you read. God the Holy Spirit will be with you helping you to see what Jesus and Father God are like (John 14:26-27).

PRAY

Holy Spirit of the Living God. Please come and fill my heart.
In Jesus' name.

Day 04

PRAYER SPACE

Here's an opportunity to take some time to think what the words "Delight yourself in the Lord" actually mean. Choose one style of wording, put on a worship song and use the page opposite to slowly write it out, whilst thinking deeply about what it means.

Take delight in the Lord

Take delight in the Lord

Take delight in the Lord

TAKE DELIGHT IN THE LORD

Take delight in the Lord

Take delight in the Lord

TAKE DELIGHT IN THE LORD

TAKE DELIGHT IN THE LORD

WORRIES ROLLED AWAY
Day 05

Commit your way to the LORD; trust in Him

I *have* to tell you something that happened to some friends as they drove to a big event one evening. Parking was an issue, so they parked their car in a street within walking distance of the concert.

As they walked to the venue, they came across a man whose car had broken down. He was attempting to bump start his car by pushing it to get it moving. Once he had the car in motion, he planned to jump into the driver's seat and turn the key whilst letting the clutch go, to "bump" the car into life. To both push and drive is a tricky job to do on your own, so our friends stopped and all four of them surrounded the car and began pushing. It was hard work to start with, as they had a hill to contend with. Yet soon they reached the highest point of the hill and the pushing became easier as they went down the road.

Then, as the car gathered speed, one of the friends noticed that the man whose car it was, was not in the driver's seat. He had been pushing and decided that now was a good time to get to the steering wheel.   Unfortunately, the car had now gathered too much momentum and the owner was struggling to keep up. Running at full speed, the man could not reach the handle of the car door as the pace of the car was greater than the pace he could muster. The car continued to gather speed even though everyone had stopped pushing. Then, hurtling driverless down the road, the car crashed into a lamp post at the bottom of the hill!

We read the words "Commit your way to the Lord," which carries the idea of rolling a burden completely away to God. Some worries we experience can completely overwhelm us, to the point of feeling hopeless; that no one is able to help us. God says here "See what I can do about it if you roll your burden on to Me; but you have to let it go." Like rolling a weight down a hill, we need to fully give God the opportunity to help us. Do you ever find that part a bit tricky? In a weird way we tend to hold on to our concerns, as worrying makes us feel like we are somehow being productive processing it on repeat in our thoughts. Actually, rather than helping, this can really weigh us down and wear us out.

❝ Commit your way to the Lord carries the idea of rolling a burden completely away to God. ❞

God has a better way. Commit your way to Him. Roll all your worries away from you and towards Him. Easier said than done? How do we do it? It's important to understand that our fears are mainly based on a potential set of circumstances that have not actually happened. We just worry that they might occur. Release to God the fear of the unknown. Remind yourself that God is always working on your behalf and that He works all things together for the good of those who love Him, according to His purposes (Romans 8). It won't end in a car crash!

God who is all good and loves to give good gifts to His children is influencing the details of your future. So tell those restless, negative thoughts about worst-case scenarios to be quiet and instead see how you are being well looked after by One who has not forgotten you.

Committing our way to God, means taking on His way of doing things. We have to release our preferences of how we would like things to turn out, to let God work His better solution. Maybe you just want that bully to move school, or at least go down with a stomach bug! Perhaps God wants to turn a bad situation around into a better outcome than you could ever imagine! He says to you "Leave it with Me. Let it go. Trust Me." Sometimes the best way of showing our trust is to take the decision to refuse to worry. So when a worrisome thought pops into your head reject it, even say out loud, "Go away. I'm trusting Jesus with this one!"

PRAY

Lord Jesus. Thank You that I don't have to carry my worries. You carried all of my sin as well as my sorrows and burdens on the cross. I choose to live in the freedom you paid for me. I give you my concerns, I let them roll over into Your care. I'm trusting You with them all! I love You!

Day 05

PRAYER SPACE

Left Hand

Place your left hand on this page and draw around it. Then whilst talking to God, think of the difficulties that you want to give over to God and write them inside the hand drawing. (If you don't want to write them why not put in initials instead?). Then as you pray, thank God that He is your refuge and hand them to Him.

When you've done this, turn over to the next page ⇒

PRAYER SPACE

Place your right hand on this page and draw around it.
Thank God that you can trust Him when you are having to deal
with uncertain times. Now ask Him for His help and protection
Then inside your hand drawing, write down what you would
like to receive from Him.

RIGHT WAYS REWARDED
Day 06

*Commit your way to the LORD; trust in him and he will do this:
He will make your righteous reward shine like the dawn, your
vindication like the noonday sun.*

I remember the day I had a fight at school. I believe I was in my third year of High School and it was just a random day in a normal week. We had entered the Science lab and as I went to sit at my work bench I was approached by this lad in my class. He was in my face, accusing me of stuff and he was being a jerk. I put out my hand to ease him away from invading my personal space. That's when it came; out of nowhere, a boxer's fist to the side of my head. My glasses were knocked across the room and in that split-second I acted in like manner. Launching into the blurry figure in front of me, I swung a right-hander into his eye. What followed was a lot of flailing about, with me fending off punches and trying to make mine count. At this point the Science teacher had seen enough and stepped in to stop the fight.

Immediately the Head Teacher was called in and an investigation was started to find out the cause of this incident. Both of us were taken out of the class and questioned by the Head. Before the lesson was over, I was returned to the Science class (to cheers from my class mates), whilst my opponent was excluded temporarily from school.

You might be thinking "Wow. That was swift justice!" How come the other lad was punished, whilst I was let off? The reason I was cleared of wrongdoing so quickly, was because the other guy just happened to be the school bully. I don't doubt that the bully would have lied and made me out to be the offending party; yet it was my version of events that was believed and trusted. It all has to do with this Hebrew word "*sidqeka*" that we find in the part we read, which is best translated into English as "righteous reward." This word means two things at the same time: being innocent of accusations brought, which in turn brings the favour of God. The benefits of living a life of integrity and honesty mean that when false accusations are brought against the innocent, God will see to it that the truth of our actions will be revealed. Those who have been unjustly charged with wrongdoing will be awarded God's extra assistance.

We read the words *"Commit your way to the Lord; trust Him and He will do this: He will make your righteous reward shine like the dawn, your vindication like the noonday sun."* Are you trying to defend yourself in a dispute where you know you have not done what they are accusing you of? Are you being misrepresented or have lies been spread about you? You might not always be able to stop the lies or win the fight; but much like the sun is brightest in the middle of the day, God will see that the truth will out and in due time your integrity will shine for all to see.

> **❝Committing our way to the Lord involves relying on God to bring about the justice that we need.❞**

Maybe someone has done you wrong. You've gone through the right channels to report what's happening to those who need to know about it; but afterwards you feel you need to do more than that. "If only everyone knew my side of the story, all my problems would be solved!" We feel that if every person hears our side, about the way "so and so" has behaved, everything will be okay. It's natural to care what everyone else thinks about us, as we wonder if our reputation is going to be harmed by misleading remarks or false stories going around. God wants to reassure you that you don't need to go about setting the story straight with the entire world. Committing our way to the Lord involves relying on God to bring about the justice that we need. In due time, God will ensure that the genuine and the false will be seen for what they are. This requires a good degree of patience from you, as you trust what God has put into place to help you. Believe that God sees your innocence and will ensure your cause will see the justice you deserve when it matters most.

PRAY

Father God. You know the injustice I've experienced. I thank You, that You are a God of justice! Help me to honour Your ways and not to copy the ways of those who use lies and deception. I place my trust in You, that You will make the truth come out. I trust You to defend me. In Jesus name!

Day 06

commit your way
TO THE LORD; TRUST IN
him and he will do this:
HE WILL MAKE
your righteous reward
SHINE LIKE THE DAWN,
your vindication like the noonday sun.

MOTIVATED BY IMPATIENCE?
Day 07

Be still before the LORD and wait patiently for Him; do not fret when people succeed in their ways, when they carry out their wicked schemes.

If queuing were a sport, I would be really bad at it. You might say, "Really? In whose world could queuing ever be considered competitive? Isn't it just standing behind another person, who is then standing behind another person??" Well if darts can be considered a sport and chess is, then isn't it just a mix of the two? If you're anything like me at a multiple till checkout, although it appears that you're waiting patiently, inside you're thinking "I must strive to select the shortest, most efficient queueing opportunity!"

To achieve the goal of getting to the car park before everyone else, you have to become a little bit nosey. Which people are going to cost you precious seconds? Could it be those with expensive wine? They'll have a security tag, as will fragrances and electrical items. Many a till operator has struggled to locate or remove security tags with speed. Adults with small children, have additional complications unrelated to their shopping. Spillages, tantrums, forgotten items and minor injuries are all potential time hazards. Who else should we avoid? Whilst we honour and respect our elders, there are reasons

37

why standing behind the elderly in a queue is going to take longer. What am I talking about? Vouchers. Our senior citizens are the most money savvy people around and have saved up their money off vouchers for moments like these. Once located, it's a given that at least one voucher will have unfairly small print disqualifying its use or be impossible to scan. Be ready for a long conversation to follow!

It's easy to become impatient in moments like these; and if you're anything like me, you'll switch queues to get through quicker. Yet, nine times out of ten, a queue switch will result in being delayed even longer! Sometimes we have difficulty in waiting for God's answers to our prayers. It can be similar to the feeling of standing in a queue where nothing appears to be progressing; at which point we begin to compare our plight to how others are doing. Then, motivated by our impatience, we begin to see if we can make our own way instead of waiting for God's timing.

Do you feel unfairly treated? It's tempting to allow fear to scare us into acting out of character. Our brains can be wired with a fear mentality that can make us second guess the thoughts of others. Have you ever acted stupidly, because you misunderstood what was going on? Maybe you're asking God to help you find love, but nothing seems to be happening? Unfortunately, impatience can lead us to make rash or ill-thought-out decisions. Sometimes there just isn't a short-cut to God's purposes.

You'd think the words *"Be still before the Lord,"* simply mean "Be quiet and pray"; but it also refers to how we act. *"Be still!"* deliberately follows on from *"Commit your way to the Lord,"* saying once you have rolled your troubles over to God, it's time to demonstrate your confidence in Him. You don't need to stress in the waiting or think you are completely responsible for how life will turn out. When God is involved, He makes sure that you'll have what you need. Some things will depend on whether the timing is right, or whether you are ready for what you're asking for. You might find that when you next read your Bible, God lets you into part of the secret of what is coming next in your life. This is His way of drawing out your trust in Him. It's in that quiet place with God that your confidence in Him has been built. So be confident in God's wisdom as well as His solution, by resisting the urge to do what your fears are telling you.

> **" Sometimes there just isn't a short-cut to God's purposes. "**

At times, we can actually make life more stressful than it needs to be; especially when we're checking on how we're doing compared to others. There's a value in the process of waiting, when it's done in partnership with God. He honours patience practiced, as we obey what's written in His word. Good things are in store for those who wait for Him.

PRAY

Father God. Help me to see your solutions for the things that I need help with, instead of trying to make my own way. In Jesus' name.

Day 07

DISCONTENTED?
Day 8

*"Refrain from anger and turn from wrath;
do not fret—it leads only to evil." (Psalm 37:8)*

A while ago I noticed that my boys were having a few speed issues whilst playing Minecraft on their PC. I couldn't understand why they had glitches and lag when playing, so I decided to Google it! After not very long, I realised that they were using the 32-bit version on a 64-bit machine. That must be it! So as all good dads do, I sprang into action, got the computer out and downloaded the necessary 64bit Java software to make it all work.

I tested it all out and found that the frames per second were much higher, with no lag and all was well. Woo hoo!! I do admit to feeling like a bit of a hero! That was until we shut down the computer... As I clicked on the start menu, an error message came up. The start menu was refusing to work. In fact, I could do very little apart from turn the computer off. After switching on and off multiple times I realised that maybe I had not come to the rescue after all!

Following several long hours on Google, trying out various solutions, I came to the conclusion there was only one thing to do... the dreaded "reset to factory default." Effectively, this returns the computer to the state that we bought it in. Unfortunately, we'd lose all the apps and files. Hmm... Well? Did I do it? Of course! Don't worry, it only took me 2 days to get everything back to normal!

I'm sure you've experienced the situation of having a device that goes slow after an update, or a computer that just gets filled up with stuff, making every task take forever. Maybe you've checked your storage and seen that there's plenty of storage space and you can't figure it out. As you've just heard, I'm not an expert, but there's probably an app conflict or something working overtime which reduces the processing speed, producing that annoying lag.

You know, much like computers, when we are processing a lot of worrisome thoughts around in our heads it produces a kind of lag. We'll be distracted, not our happy selves and feeling sluggish. The bit we have read here today tells us that fretting only leads in one direction. It's not a good direction. Fretting produces a build-up of stuff that makes us stressed. This can lead to all kind of things like anger, self-harm, broken relationships and bad habits (to name but a few).

This is the third "Do not fret," that we've come across in this Psalm. Maybe you feel that the words "Don't worry," just aren't enough to deal with your problem, yet what worry does is to put our focus on the wrong things. Not only does it wallow in the problem, but more importantly it believes the "worst-case-scenarios" that our mind has come up with. By worrying, we are placing our faith in the enemy's plans for our lives. Instead, God wants us to change our perspective and see the plans that He has for our lives. We use the factory default button to return back to when things were working well. So, it's worth asking, "What is the cause of my discontentment?" Often it will be something that hasn't actually happened yet. It could be that we are feeling afraid of something that threatens us in some way. The enemy loves to make us fearful about things that never actually happen.

> **❝** By worrying, we are placing our faith
> in the enemy's plans for our lives. **❞**

It's time to change your default actions. If something doesn't go to plan, rather than trusting in the enemy's plans for your life, trust in the greater capacity of your loving Heavenly Father to see you through your difficulties. Maybe you react in a certain negative way at the first sight of trouble. Seize that moment and say to yourself "The Lord says 'Do not fret!!'" Allow God to take charge, rather than the enemy.

PRAY

Father God, thank You that You have this thing covered. Please lead me to see that my worries are misplaced and will draw me toward evil, but my faith in You is always well placed and will lead me toward good!" In Jesus Name!

Day 08

PRAYER SPACE

THANKS

THINGS GOD HAS DONE

GOD YOU ARE

in my life you have...

i trust that you are:

*what i love
about you is*

HELP ME WITH...

I devote this to You:

JUSTICE AND MERCY
Day 09

For those who are evil will be destroyed,
but those who hope in the LORD will inherit the land.

I have you tell you about the time me and my friends decided to film a funny sketch on the church grounds. Months before we had created a comedy video that went down a storm, so we thought it was only right to create a sequel. We decided on a ninja theme for our video, so one of the props I bought were some balaclavas from the local motorbike shop. You know the kind of thing, a black facemask, which has a big hole for the eyes.

Well we went to film the scene. My two friends were waiting around the corner, ready to charge towards the camera wearing the balaclavas and brandishing baseball bats. Unfortunately, whilst we had a small delay with the camera, a lady going into the back hall noticed my two friends and thought they were planning a raid. So she called the Police.

Meanwhile me and my friends carried on filming, unaware that actions were underway at the local Police station. After filming outside, we went into the church to carry on filming, when there was a knock at the door. I answered the door to find a Policeman standing there. "Is everything okay?" he asked. I told him (unconvincingly) that we were fine. He then went on to ask me about a report of some males acting suspiciously. I realised he was referring to our ninja outfits and explained that we were doing a comedy film, to which he replied that we were only five minutes away from triggering an armed response unit! Just imagine what the headlines of the local papers would have been!

We've previously read an instruction not to fret when people's bad ways are succeeding, as the temptation is to think that this is all there is. Yesterday we were encouraged to be patient. Why? Much like my friends and me were blissfully unaware that a Police unit was springing into action, so God is working behind-the-scenes on behalf of justice. We'll often feel there's cause for worry if we're not taking on board this truth. God's purposes will come to pass in ways we could never expect! Why is this true? Because God has an inheritance in store for you! He wants you to partner in His ways to enjoy the journey to this inheritance and to live in His peace. So it's important to put away the desire to return evil for evil, as that is partnering with the enemy rather than with God; and we know that such actions cause our lives to wither.

We are told that the plans of the wicked will come to nothing when brought against us, because *"those who hope in the Lord will inherit the land"* (v9). Hope here actually means having confidence in someone. It's not like "I hope it won't rain today," like an unpredictable "I hope so." It's a confidence placed in someone. When we're afraid, our fears only believe in negative outcomes. However, when we start to place our confidence in who God is, we begin to demonstrate faith. This brings a great reward. God's reward is something He has been preparing for you. He plans for you to enjoy His help each day through a life which is activated by faith. It was His plan in the first place to work for your good according to His purposes (Romans 8:28). You can be confident that God has good things in store for you.

> **"** It's important to put away the desire to return evil for evil, as that is partnering with the enemy rather than with God. **"**

Whilst we will have times of trouble where people are against us, we have a God who wants to partner with us. As you trust in the Lord and do good, delighting in Him, you are enjoying that partnership that God intended to have with you. You will find yourself in the place that the Lord has provided for you. Jesus wants you to have His peace in this journey of life with Him. So have confidence in His unseen ways, enjoy His presence with you and expect to see the good things he has in store for you as his son or daughter.

PRAY

Father God. Thank You that You provide a table for me in the presence of my enemies. Thank you that I can look forward to the good things that you have in store for me! In Jesus's name.

Day 09

FOR THOSE WHO
are evil
WILL BE
destroyed,
BUT
those who
HOPE IN THE
lord will
INHERIT
the land.

HOPE'S ANTHEM

Day 10

A little while, and the wicked will be no more;
though you look for them, they will not be found.

There seems to be something quite satisfying about watching the demise of villains in a film. You've been on a journey with your hero and seen the injustice and evil they have had to face. You have also followed the villain and seen his evil plans unfold as he moves toward his aim of causing chaos, claiming power, wealth and influence at the same time. But finally, after a long battle, the hero triumphs and the villain's power base is removed. In fact, at the end the villain looks quite pathetic really, when his mask is removed, his powers have been stripped away and his army is defeated. Now, he is nothing; and we maybe wonder why he seemed like such an impossible foe to beat.

Sometimes we can build people up in our minds, viewing them as having such power that they are untouchable or unbeatable. It may be that there is a spiritual enemy partnering with them, using manipulation, intimidation and lies to give them their place. Yet, you and I have the Lord God Almighty working on our behalf! There will be times when evil attempts to usurp God's plans, but what we are reading today is that any such attempts to steal the inheritance that God intends to give us is a lost cause.

When we look forward in life, we don't know what is going to happen next, we don't know what tomorrow will bring. There's a degree of uncertainty about the future. As we read the words *"though you look for them, they will not be found,"* these are from someone who is an old man, telling of his experience, looking back. He's giving us two perspectives, one which tells how it wasn't long before something happened; he is also telling us that this change will happen suddenly. It's like a narrator is telling the story of your life, whilst reassuringly promising that they will carefully watch the place of the bad guy and then one day, he or she won't be in your life anymore.

The end result is not in doubt. Why are we being told this? Sometimes we need a reason to be patient, to hold fast. The temptation of the enemy is to make us believe we've already lost, that we may as well give up. That's what the enemy wants you and me to do. Instead, be patient, because the Lord is working where you and I can't always see. We don't always see how vulnerable the enemy actually is. Like a troll hiding behind a computer screen, pretending to be a criminal mastermind, the enemy works away at our fears. However, a knock at the door from the authorities changes everything. The very last thing the enemy wants us to do is to expose his deception, because it takes away his power. When God shines his light of truth on the situation, it exposes the secret ways of evil which thrive on being hidden.

> **❝ The temptation of the enemy is to make us believe we've already lost, that we may as well give up. ❞**

We're encouraged here to patiently wait for God's solution to present itself, rather than trying to make our own way. Patience can be tough, because waiting for the solution can feel like carrying your heavy school bag, full of books. It's dragging you down and taking away your strength. Yet even in the waiting, we can hand over the burden of our concerns about what may be ahead. Whilst we can't see what God is doing, our patience involves trusting that He will work things out in his way. This can actually be like a weight lifted off! We can't speed up God's plans, we can only slow them down by trying to sort it all out on our own! This doesn't mean that you should do nothing to help the situation. When you're partnering with God, you'll enjoy His peace in times of trouble. Although there may be a waiting time, you will look back and see the schemes of the wicked have come to nothing, as the beautiful purposes of God are revealed.

PRAY

Father God. Thank You that You are a good God, who hates the evil things that people do. I know that whilst evil is on the earth, You are working to defeat it forever. I ask for patience in my struggle and for my mind and my heart to stick closely to You. I'm looking to You to help me through. May the evil deeds of my enemies be discovered and dealt with. In Jesus' name!

Day 10

PRAYER SPACE

Here's an opportunity to contemplate those words of Psalm 42:11 "Put your hope in God, for I will yet praise Him." As you can see there is some lettering below. Why not use these letters to write out Psalm 42:11 on the opposite page. It's worth putting on some Christian worship music whilst you do this. Be open to God speaking to you through what you do.

Aa Bb Cc Dd

Ee Ff Gg Hh

Ii Jj Kk Ll

Mm Nn Oo Pp

Qq Rr Ss Tt

Uu Vv Ww Xx

Yy Zz

PRAYER SPACE

INHERITANCE
Day 11

But the meek will inherit the land and enjoy peace and prosperity.

Have you ever heard of those whose job it is to find the long-lost relatives of those who have passed away? People called *Heir Hunters* step in to investigate when someone with an estate dies without having written a last will and testament. Research into the family tree of a person can lead to locating relatives who have a legal right to inherit any money or property owned. Just imagine, that moment when you get a knock at the door and are told that you're a descendant of a millionaire and you get to share in their wealth. So why would you deserve to get the money? It's only because you are related that you are entitled to it. Discovering that you have an inheritance is an exciting and potentially life changing moment. It opens up a world of new possibilities, from buying your own place, to having the means to set up your own business! With such potential for opportunity, it's worth discovering what the inheritance that God has for us is all about.

We're told that "the meek will inherit the land." For a moment, let's assume you and I are meek. What does it mean to inherit the land? The land is an ancient concept that is found in Genesis 12:1 and develops through the Old Testament. It basically takes the idea of a place of safety where you can live, enjoying God's favour and where his purposes will be fulfilled in your life. This is what God promised Abram (also known as Abraham), who responded by doing what God asked of him. An inheritance is a gift that not just anyone gets. You have to be related! It's a destiny promised to you that you have not earned or achieved by your own efforts. The phrase "inherit the land," has to do with something we're given from God that is enjoyed when we live daily in partnership with Him. It's His plans being fulfilled in our lives.

> **❝An inheritance is a gift that not just anyone gets. You have to be related! ❞**

What exactly do "the meek" inherit? The rest of the verse gives us a big clue! Amongst other things, it includes enjoying "peace and prosperity." Ok, so the word prosperity has been misused by some Christian preachers over the years, but here, the original Hebrew word actually means to have more than enough! And before we get too spiritual about it and just imagine that this relates to unknown spiritual stuff, the prosperity word here is actually talking about things that bring enjoyment and comfort – material blessings. Things we need each day, like food and a place to live, as well as those we enjoy, such as friendships and a job we love. God loves to provide things that we find useful too, like books or tech, puzzle cubes, a bike, musical instrument, or whatever! But there's more! "To inherit" also means to receive moral and spiritual favour. What we have spoken about are things given by God. So these will be good things. In addition to these, God wants us to enjoy His spiritual favour. This is about living in partnership and relationship with Him.

He wants to make your times with him come alive. He wants you to hear His voice and know that He is close by. He wants you to experience what happens when you involve Him in your day-to-day decisions. As you do this, you will enjoy peace in your life and discover God's purposes for your future, which will be greater than any financial riches.

So would you call yourself a meek person? A meek person is someone who lives their life in partnership with God. It doesn't mean they live a perfect life, but that they have submitted their lives to God and live obediently, respecting God and His ways. As you do this, Jesus says you will be blessed! Take a look at Matthew 5:5. Sound familiar? We can't earn God's favour, but we can certainly enjoy it when we wholeheartedly follow Him.

PRAY

Father God. Thank You that I have an inheritance from You, as a daughter or son in your house! I want to honour You with my life. Help me not to ignore the ways that You want to change me. May my attitude be one that selflessly lives for You. You are my King. Thank You for the many blessings that You have in store for me, as I journey with You in my life! In Jesus' name!

Day 11

FACING AGRESSION
Day 12

The wicked plot against the righteous
and gnash their teeth at them;

Ever heard of the phrase "fight fire with fire"? It's the theme of a song by 80's heavy metal band Metallica, that has to do with how to respond when someone is hostile towards you. The idea of the phrase is that if someone is aggressive toward you, be aggressive back, fight fire with fire, burn them up before they burn you. Well, I have a friend who is a firefighter; she would advise a very different strategy. She would tell you that a more successful strategy would be to fight fire with water!

In the bit we read, we're given a picture of aggression, where evil people are deliberately targeting followers of God. Why are they doing this? The book of Revelation gives us a clue! It tells us in Revelation 12:12-17, that God's enemy the devil "is filled with fury" and goes off to make war against God's people. There is sometimes an evil spiritual power behind the scenes, trying to motivate people to harm the righteous. Using this anger, the devil turns people against the followers of Jesus. The picture language used in the verse we read (Psalm 37:12) of gnashing teeth, is of someone intent on conflict, to attack and do harm. However, the good news is that as part of our inheritance in God, we have a power to overcome such aggression and therefore diffuse those being hostile toward us. That power is called prayer!

In the face of the haters, a different approach to hate is required. Fight fire with water. Water is not the opposite of fire; it's not being passive in the face of aggression. It is still fighting, but in a very different way. So then, we need to discover what God's way of doing things is. Talk to Him about it; but more than that, give God lots of opportunities to talk back to you. Be really open and ready to hear Him speaking as you read the Bible. Be sensitive to the possibility of God speaking to you through other people, or through the picture language of your dreams as you sleep. Tune into God for His wisdom. Through discovering God's thoughts, you'll understand more of how to fight with water.

"We need to discover what God's way of doing things is."

What is the water we fight with then? As we've said, prayer is a weapon that God has given you to fight the enemy. *First* of all, Jesus wants us to pray for our human enemies! I know that's probably the last thing you'd want to do, but this facilitates God's way of working (Matt 5:44). God is totally good and fair. He will exact the appropriate revenge as we follow His way of doing things. *Second*, release to God all the bad feelings that you have towards your enemy. If you hold on to hate, you'll become bitter and it will eat you up on the inside. Again, this is difficult, but it's God's route to being truly happy. Let God help you with this. *Third*, ask God to give you wisdom for what to pray. Targeted prayer against the enemy sees powerful results. Then *last* of all, ask for God's supernatural help to provide for your every need in this situation. Ask Him to help you with all the things you can't do. Then, as you see God helping you, appreciate it. Even the small things that happen that you needed and didn't even ask for; take time to thank God for His help. It might be as simple as a friend sharing their food with you at lunchtime which leads to you feeling supported, or your aggressor being held up in some way, making them unable to cause you problems. As you trust God to help you with the things you can't make happen, you will see Him working in more and more amazing ways.

Fighting fire with fire will only make more trouble. Instead, fighting with the water of prayer will produce some life-changing results that could never have come about by responding in aggression.

PRAY

Father God. Thank You for going before me and providing things that have helped me through my day. Your love truly does not end or fail. I know that living for you may increase my enemies, but with You I can approach today and tomorrow with hope. Father. Give me strength in the face of difficult situations and may the threats my enemies come to nothing. In Jesus' name!

Day 12

PRAYER SPACE

Jesus. Thank You for what you suffered for me

Consider what Jesus has done

Help me to understand what it cost You, Jesus.

What do you want to tell Jesus about?

Thank You that we can face tough times together.

With You I can face anything.

What are your concerns for the future?

LAUGHING OUT LOUD
Day 13

but the Lord laughs at the wicked,
for he knows their day is coming.

Have you ever laughed so much that you couldn't breathe? I remember being on mission with some friends in Estonia. Some of us were taking a much-needed rest, whilst some of the girls were painting a three-metre-long banner which was going to advertise a kid's club coming up that week.

As we kicked a football around outside, the girls had finished their artwork and began carrying the long banner to a nearby car. Not the easiest of tasks with the paint still drying, but they decided now was the time to move it and it couldn't be rolled up. Well, at the moment of transportation, a long ball pass was mis-kicked and like a scene in a film, everything was reduced to slow-motion, whilst we all held our breath. The girls stopped, eyes turning towards the incoming object. There was no stopping the flight of the ball and as it decreased in speed. Dropping inches short of the banner, it hit the muddiest puddle you have ever seen! The resulting splash sent muddy water all over the banner. The girls stood there holding the banner, frozen in time, aghast at the misfortune that had befallen their showpiece. The momentary silence ended, as we fell about

62

laughing so much that it actually hurt (the girls did laugh too, eventually). The scene was just too funny! Ever laughed like that? You know, where at that moment there's not a care in the world!

Yesterday, we read about how to deal with the threats of evil people. You're just going about your business when you come across someone with a bad attitude who has decided to take it all out on you. Nothing to laugh about here. How is it that God laughs at those who threaten his people? When the threat of something bad befalling us comes to our attention, the last thing we want to do is laugh. But think for a moment *why* we get stressed. Some of the time we have made our problems more serious than they actually are. It is only an idea, an intention, a plot. Sometimes we take life too seriously and can fall into the trap of making things or people bigger than they actually are. A tiny speck of dust on the wrong part of a lens can be very annoying, but it is still only a speck. God laughs at their intentions, because in comparison to Him, they are just a speck, a weak plant which is here today and tomorrow is no more. We can often stress about the small things, when God wants us to laugh, because he knows how He's working and how things are going to turn out. When you're laughing, you're not stressed. In that moment worry and fear have no effect. God laughs at their plans! He's in charge and working on your behalf!

I often wonder whether some situations in my life might have played out differently, if I had just said something humorous at the opportune moment. You know, those stressful moments where everyone has gotten too serious about something that doesn't really matter, or when someone is trying to control the atmosphere by using intimidation. I'm sure you've been there, where the atmosphere in a room has turned super-serious and people are getting unnecessarily heavy about something quite trivial. They just need a little perspective to see how small the issue actually is and saying something appropriately funny at the right moment (with a cheeky smile) can calm the situation like the diffusing of an unexploded bomb.

> **"** God laughs at their plans! He's in charge and working on your behalf! **"**

God is not worried. He is at peace. Therefore, why should we get all worked up? When you tell God about your difficulties, read His words too, so that you can then see things from His perspective. You'll soon be able to laugh about the small things and look forward to your future with hope.

PRAY

Mighty God, King of my life. Thank You that You are my Father and that I have an inheritance prepared for me, because of what Jesus has done. I have a good future ahead of me and I know that Your plans for me are good. As I go through tough times when I'm threatened by the evil schemes of others, cause me to laugh and trust that your plans are stronger. In Jesus' name!

Day 13

PRAYER SPACE

Have you ever said to Jesus, "Lord. I'm here. I want to meet with You. I'll wait for You. I'll be with you as long as You want"?

Why not come to Jesus with that attitude now?

Inviting the Holy Spirit
Jesus wants you to receive the Holy Spirit (John 14:15-17).
Ask the Holy Spirit to show you more of Jesus and Father God.

Waiting for the Holy Spirit

Jesus said to wait for the Holy Spirit (Acts 1:4-5).
Ask the Holy Spirit to fill you with God's presence.

What is God saying to you?

Ask the Lord to show you something more about what He's like.

Ask the Lord to show you something He loves about you.

What is your response to Him?

FIGHTING AGAINST GOD
Day 14

*The wicked draw the sword and bend the bow
to bring down the poor and needy, to slay those whose ways are
upright. But their swords will pierce their own hearts,
and their bows will be broken.*

I remember the day when the bank I was working in was raided by masked gunmen. It was a small branch located in Stepney, East London and being on the Commercial Road, it also made for an easy getaway for potential criminals. I was working about 10 feet from the cashier, when I heard this shouting and banging. I turned around expecting to see an angry customer, when I saw two men wearing balaclavas and carrying sawn-off shotguns.

This was a new situation for me and I just thought everyone would duck for cover under the nearest desk, instead we just all pretty much stood and watched. The casher lady was handing out bundles of money, starting with £5 notes, pushing them through the slot. It was weird seeing a cashier do that, as they normally count out notes very carefully before handing anything over. Such strange circumstances were only possible in a bank because the men were wielding guns. The fact that we were standing behind bullet-proof glass and that we didn't know if the weapons were loaded or not, didn't change the need to hand over the money. People were at risk and the men were very aggressive.

On TV and in the movies, if a person is holding a gun and pointing it at someone it is considered a big threat; and in ancient times, both sword and bow would have had a similar effect. So far, we've been considering how easy it is to fret about a person or situation that is hypothetical, it hasn't happened. Here, we read of bad people prepared to attack *"The wicked draw the sword and bend the bow"* and speaks of immediate and present things that are making us feel unsafe. When we are encouraged not to fret, it isn't saying "you're just imagining it," or, "it doesn't matter," or "everything is just fine." The fretting we are experiencing is acknowledged here with a set of very real circumstances. Yet just because the issue we fear begins to play out in real life, it isn't a sign that God has forgotten us.

Sometimes God uses challenging situations to bring about a victory that we need. The stories of greatest victory are often those where a person or group of people are faced with the greatest difficulty. Don't give up! Keep going! Don't be disheartened when the challenges that you fear, present themselves. God has not left you. He wants to partner with you in the challenges you are facing. Continue to trust Him. A wise person once said "If you are going through hell, keep going!"[2] As Christians we are protected by God, yet this doesn't mean we'll not face suffering, hard times or challenges. God will not leave us in these times. In fact, He will be very close by, ready to help us through the hard times, providing what we need when we need it to get through.

❝ Sometimes God uses challenging situations to bring about a victory that we need. ❞

In the bit we just read, God assures us that He will bring justice for your cause for "their swords will pierce their own hearts." The very weapons used to attack you, will be used by God for your victory. Unfair words and lies being used to attack you will be used to bring down your attackers! Those who threaten and plot with evil in mind against the righteous, will end up targeting themselves by mistake. It's because those who attack us are actually picking a fight with God. They are challenging God's inheritance for you and He takes this very personally! He will fight for you. He will turn the actions of your unjust attackers into the very thing which will defeat their attack. God will take away their control over you and rescue you as you continue to trust and follow His guidance.

PRAY

Father God. Help me not to be fearful in the difficult situations that I am facing. Thank You that You will be close by and with me through the worst of times. Thank You that no one can stand in the way of Your purposes being fulfilled in my life. I am Yours forever! In Jesus' name!

Day 14

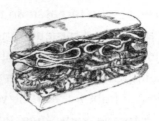

RICH OR POOR?
Day 15

*Better the little that the righteous have
than the wealth of many wicked;*

A while back in our youth meeting, we posed a question to everyone, which seemed easy to answer at the start, but turned out to be a bit more tricky than we thought. The question was, "Does money buy you happiness?" Folks then had to move to one side of the room if they thought "yes" and the other side of the room if it was "no." Almost instantly, everyone moved over to the "no" side, to say that money does not buy happiness. Yet there was one person who chose to stand on the "yes" side. What would you say?

The person standing on the "yes" side (saying money does buy happiness) was asked, "Tell us why did you choose that side?" Her reply was this, "If you are poor and hungry and you are given money to eat food, in that moment, the money you have used has brought you happiness." She went on to say that although it can buy happiness, the happiness that money buys only has a temporary effect. It doesn't last forever.

Money isn't evil, but there are times when it is used so selfishly by the rich that it would have been better for them to not have had it at all. For a start, wealth comes with its own set of responsibilities and challenges! I'm sure you've noticed those with great riches abusing their status and power to control or gain advantage over others. Perhaps you've seen pictures of the super-rich with outrageously expensive items that they have bought for themselves. A rich person might say that they have the right to spend their wealth selfishly or wastefully if they want to. But does having lots of money not also come with some responsibility too? What would you do if you found yourself owning millions of pounds? Would you treat yourself to a Lamborghini? Or would you use it to build a school in Uganda?

We can easily become blinded by the lure of selfish living. This can put us at risk of offending the justice of God. Take for example the rich oil corporation that puts profit ahead of the health and living conditions of local indigenous peoples. God's promise is that those who use their wealth in evil ways will find no prosperity in their future. God's justice works in two ways: He will judge as guilty those responsible for such suffering and He will also work on behalf of the innocent who call on Him.

" Wealth can lead to the kind of thinking that doesn't need God. "

When we honour God with whatever we have, it draws His favour. This brings freedom to living that money can't buy. Although you may have little, you have access to God's ways of working which don't depend upon what you have accumulated. In His kingdom, small mustard seeds produce enormous trees, a boy's lunch feeds thousands and a hopeless night of fishing turns into a record haul.

His is a kingdom where a prayer of thanks to God for what we have multiplies to meet our needs and so much more! If we think we already have what we need, it will be much easier to live independently from God and miss out on some amazing things. The righteous have access to God's storehouse, which is by far greater than any person on earth could own. God is so generous and loves to share what He has with those He loves.

If you desire to be rich, remember that it has a danger which you'll have to navigate. Wealth can lead to the kind of thinking that doesn't need God. It's easier to become self-sufficient and to forget God when you have all you need. Jesus wants our relationship with Him to be one of full dependence on Him. So ask Him to help supply your needs, whether great or small and He will! When we fully depend on God, we have access to the limitless resources of heaven. Your future is more secure and your opportunities are greater, when you have a little with God than millions without Him.

PRAY

Father God. Thank You for all the ways that You provided for me yesterday. Thank You that You want me to ask for your help and to depend on You in every situation. I ask that You would teach me how to rely on You and show me more of what You are like. Let me be generous to others with the generosity that I receive from You. In Jesus' name!

Day 15

BETTER THE
little that
THE RIGHTEOUS
have than
THE WEALTH
of many wicked;

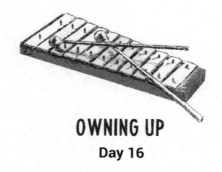

OWNING UP
Day 16

for the power of the wicked will be broken,
but the LORD upholds the righteous.

I was having a bad day at school. On a normal day, a fail like this isn't even going to be noticed, everyone goes about their business and gets on with their day. However, on a bad day, it ends up getting your whole class into trouble and leaves you wondering how something so small can escalate into such a major incident. Well. We were in a music lesson. I hated music as a subject, because I was no good at it and today was a perfect example of my useless music "skills." We had all been given a xylophone and told to learn and practice the theme tune to the Muppets. As you can imagine, with everyone playing at once, no one could hear the notes they were playing to tell if they had the tune right. It was just the worst noise ever. The teacher obviously thought so, because he went out of the room whilst we were all practising!

Yet the scene was set for my day to get a lot worse. After about five minutes of trying to work out a tune which I had little ability to play (and even less ability to hear), I said to myself "I can't hear what I'm playing." My friend next to me said "What??" I repeated myself louder, "I can't hear what I'm playing!" I couldn't even hear my own voice, so

74

even louder I shouted "I CAN'T HEAR WHAT I'M PLAYING!!!" This was ignored by everyone around me. All except one person heard me. Oh. Who was that? You ask. Of course, it was my music teacher (who was in the other room!). He heard my voice over that horrendous noise which he instigated and thought I was being too loud. He came storming into the classroom like a man possessed. "Who was that shouting??? Nobody shouts in my class!!! Tell me who it was???"

I have to say, an aggressive tone like this doesn't naturally lend itself to a confession of any kind. To own up to a man in this state of rage would not have been a good idea. Having never seen him this mad, the consequences were unknown. So I decided to keep my mouth shut. Trying to stay chilled, I looked around the classroom to make it appear that I was wondering who it could be. Seeing no one was going to admit it, the teacher stated that unless someone owned up, we would all be getting a detention. I was sure guilt was written all over my face, but since I wasn't being outed by my friend for my offence, I was not going to risk saying a word!

I know it wasn't the crime of the century, but my choice to keep quiet caused injustice to all my innocent classmates. It's easy to think, "I'm righteous, God loves me, but he hates the unrighteous." But the thing is, without Jesus, you and I are unrighteous before God. We know that God loves the unrighteous and that He provides a way which leads to life. If taken, wicked people become righteous and enjoy the benefits of the Lord's favour. Jesus provided His life as a payment for all our wrongdoing. This is for all those who choose to love and follow Him. Yet for those who reject God, who go about their way intent on unjust deeds, they had better watch out! Maybe the "little while" mentioned in verse 10 is the time period that God affords the wicked to turn to Him. Is this why we have to wait to see the wicked get justice? The Lord is totally fair and just, but also generous to the extent that we don't deserve it.

"Jesus provided His life as a payment for all our wrongdoing. This is for all those who choose to love and follow Him.**"**

It's certainly better to own up to God and receive His forgiveness, rather than keeping quiet. He's not an angry man like my music teacher, but He is totally pure and fair; hiding from the truth cannot avoid His justice when it comes. Those who rely on violence, status, riches or influence at the expense of others are on unsteady ground. Their ability to perpetuate evil deeds will be removed. However, those whose strength is dependent on the Lord, will stand the test of time, because when it appears that we will fall, God will step in and help us.

PRAY

Father God. I hate messing up! I'm sorry when I say, do and think things that are wrong. Forgive me and help me to want to do these things less and less. Lead me close to You, make my heart pure and change me. In Jesus' name.

Day 16

PRAYER SPACE

Lord I want to know more...

What is it You are telling me about Yourself today?

How do I fit into Your plan?

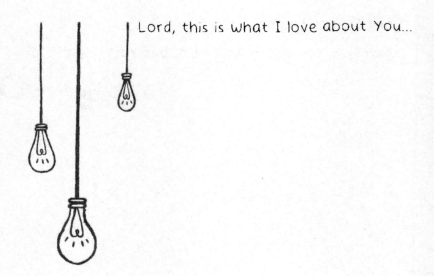

Lord, this is what I love about You...

How can I share this with others?

A SECURE LIFE
Day 17

The blameless spend their days under the LORD's care,
and their inheritance will endure forever.

I'm sure you've heard of the story that Jesus told of two builders, one wise and one foolish. The wise man selected rock as the location for his house, digging down deep for his foundation. In contrast, the foolish man thought a sandy beach would be an attractive place to build his house. Before long, the clouds turned dark and spots of rain began to appear. It continued to rain and rain as the winds blew in with thunder and lightning. Both houses began to feel the battering of the storms, beating against their roofs, walls and doors. The house built on the rock was unshakeable, no matter what the storm threw at it, it stood firm. The structure built on the sand however, began to shift with the wind, moved this way and that, pushed by its force. Eventually, the house could withstand no more. Cracks appeared and widened, before it collapsed into heap of rubble (see Luke 6:47-49).

It's a story of contrasts, with two different actions at the start, resulting in two different outcomes. Jesus likened those who listen to and obey His words to a house on a solid foundation. Such people will be kept safe when bad times or challenges come, because their lives are built on truth, having entrusted their lives to the Lord's care.

However, those who choose to live by their own moral code and wisdom, rejecting Jesus' words, will find that theirs is a way that leads to destruction. A life built on lies, no matter how genuine the intent, is one that will not last.

Today we read from Psalm 37:18 that "the blameless spend their days under the Lord's care." Much like the wise and foolish builders it makes the comparison between two opposites: those who are blameless and those who choose to do evil. If you're a follower of Jesus, you'll understand that He has taken away the blame of the wrong things you have done and forgiven you. You are innocent before God! God watches over the innocent, providing care for us through every storm and challenge.

> **"A life built on lies, no matter how genuine the intent, is one that will not last."**

So far in this Psalm, we've been encouraged not to fret or to envy those who do evil, but to trust God. Committing our way to Him will lead us to enjoy a place of safety that He has set aside for us. It's the exercising of a trust that expects God's help every day and keeps in close contact with Him. These are God's wise words for the life of faith. Following them is like building a firm foundation that will keep you secure when tough times hit. In doing so, the righteous find themselves cared for by God in the storms of life or attacks of the enemy. Though the enemy uses evil words, intimidation, violence and threat, their position is not one that will last. The Lord knows what you need and is caring for you by providing what you need to get through it all. Whether it's a good day or a bad day, the Lord Jesus is here with you. So don't think that when things are going bad that he has left you, or is busy elsewhere.

We've already talked a bit about inheritance. Although God's inheritance for us is stored for us in heaven, it begins on earth from the moment we become sons and daughters of God. The moment we believe, we come into His family and are able to enjoy the benefits of being cared for by God. This is not restricted to a far away treasure trove to be received later on in life. It's accessed through God now, today and every day after. We know that when we pass through death and into eternity, the friends of God (through Jesus His Son) will be in His presence forever. You and I can experience part of this inheritance now, since He is with us now too. There's this incredible verse in Psalm 23:5 which says, "You set a table before me in the presence of my enemies." Just like a well stocked breakfast buffet, waiting for you when you wake up, God provides for you in preparation for every battle.

PRAY

Father God. I commit to following Your ways. I know that when You are the centre of my life, things work out for the best. I know that Your loving words lead me away from foolish and destructive ways. Yours is a way that leads to a life worth living. So I choose to follow You. In Jesus' name!

Day 17

Thank God for all that you have

Thank you for the people
you have put into my life
Proverbs 17:17

Thank you for the food I have
1 Timothy 4:4

Thank you that you are always with me
Zephaniah 3:17

Thank you for your love for me
Romans 8:38-39

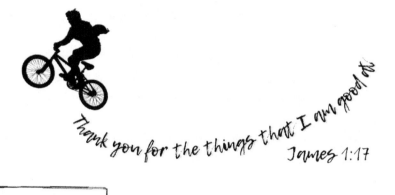

Thank you for the things that I am good at
James 1:17

Thank you for
the plans you
have for me
Proverbs 3:5-6

Thank you that you have an
inheritance stored up for me
1 Peter 1:3-4

GOD'S REFRESHING
Day 18

In times of disaster they will not wither;
in days of famine they will enjoy plenty.

Did you know that you and I are just like tomato plants? If you've ever tried to grow tomatoes, you'll know they need the sun and water. If you forget to water them, they start to wilt and look a bit sad. However, the great thing about tomato plants is that once you've given them some water, they perk up in no time and look happy again! We can be a bit like this too! I'm always telling my boys to drink more water. When I see them going around all droopy and tired, a reminder to have some water is like a miracle cure! After a few cups of water, suddenly they are revitalised and back to their normal selves again!

In the bit we read today we're shown contrasting pictures: a withered plant compared to one that is properly watered. We know that plants need water to survive and you would expect that a plant which becomes very dry in a time of famine would shrivel up and die. No hope for it to recover; but here, we're told the opposite. This plant is looking great in the day of disaster, with plenty to drink when supplies are scarce. This picture tells us what God's care for us is really like. It's worth mentioning that it doesn't say we will never experience tough times. Instead, when the challenges come along, God will be there to care for us, so that we do well when our circumstances say we should be a mess.

What sort of bad stuff are we talking about when we read the words famine and disaster? Disasters can range from turning up to an important exam half an hour late, to family break up, or even losing a loved one. Serious stuff. Jesus told us "In this life you will have trouble" (John 16:33). He suffered too. He was betrayed, rejected and lost his earthly Dad Joseph at a young age. Famines are times when resources are scarce. Whether there is less food, money or other necessary things that we need to live. Jesus promises to make sure that we do well in those times too (see Luke 12:22-32). His loving kindness to us goes against the harm that the negative circumstances might cause. Those who stay connected with Jesus will experience help coming when we need it most. So when you're up against the challenge of your life, let the Holy Spirit refresh your tired soul, so that your strength will be renewed every day. You're going to make it through.

There's actually a further meaning of the word "wither" that is used here. It also means "to be ashamed." Sometimes when we need God's help and we are facing a tricky situation, one of our fears is that our trust in God will turn out to be false. What if God doesn't come through for me? Will my faith wither because I feel disappointed that God didn't help me in the way I felt I needed? In times of trouble, it's easy to have a hard time believing that God cares. We can look at what is going on in the world and ask "Where is God?" Don't stress. Here God is giving us a definite answer to this question. God is saying that far from ignoring us in our difficulty, God is helping us through it and working on an outcome which will turn what is bad into something precious.

“ It's worth mentioning that it doesn't say
we will never experience tough times. **”**

God pays attention to our cries of pain. Actually, when we are going through good times, it can sometimes be the case that you and I might find it harder to recognise when God is close. Yet when the hardships come, it is amazing how powerfully God makes Himself known to us. When we find ourselves depending on God, because we realise that we can't help ourselves, suddenly we become aware of how much God is ready, willing and able to help us.

PRAY

Father God. Thank You that You are working everyday to care for me. You listen to every cry that I make to You. I know that my future is secure in You, both now and forever. I ask You to refresh my soul again. Make my heart strong for all the challenges that I am facing. In Jesus' name.

Day 18

in times of disaster
THEY WILL NOT WITHER;
in days of famine they
WILL ENJOY PLENTY.

SMOKED
Day 19

But the wicked will perish:
Though the LORD's enemies are like the flowers of the field,
they will be consumed, they will go up in smoke.

When I was a lad, cartoons were a good way of passing the time during the summer holidays. You had the Wacky Races, where characters raced with each other to complete a course in the fastest time, using their custom-made vehicles. Sometimes characters from other cartoons would make guest appearances to compete for a chance of the trophy. Of course, you had to watch out for the wicked duo of Dastardly and Mutley. They always had tricks up their sleeve to try and cheat their way to victory. However, if you wanted to see peril on a whole other level, the other cartoon to watch was Road Runner. This small bird with barely any meat on him was the planned meal deal of Wile E Coyote. Every ten seconds saw the evil Wile E devise a new plan to get the Road Runner; he just did not let up.

Interestingly, the Road Runner never seemed too bothered that he was literally inches away from catapulted rocks, exploding missiles and other traps that the Coyote ordered from the Acme Corporation. In fact, every attempt to harm the Road Runner backfired on Wile E

Coyote. If it was rocks, the Coyote would get squashed, if it was tar, he would get stuck and if it was explosives, he would go up in smoke. So far in reading this Psalm, we've come across eight different ways in which the demise of those intent on evil will take place. They will wither, soon die away, be destroyed, be no more, not be found, their sword will pierce their own hearts and their bows will be broken. We now read that they will perish like delicate flowers in a field and be consumed by fire, with the evidence of smoke. Sounds a lot like the misfortunes of Wile E Coyote!

What we read here today is better understood if we look back a few verses to read verses 18, 19 and 20 together.

18 The blameless spend their days under the LORD's care, and their inheritance will endure forever. 19 In times of disaster they will not wither; in days of famine they will enjoy plenty. 20 But the wicked will perish: Though the LORD's enemies are like the flowers of the field, they will be consumed, they will go up in smoke.

We're told that there's a difference between the blameless and the wicked and their futures. Those who build their lives on the words of Jesus find themselves standing firm in times of difficulty, whereas those who don't will crumble. Often evil people are arrogant, in your face and violent, which gives off an illusion of strength. Yet this is not the full story. God is saying, "Look at your enemy. They are actually fragile like a flower. Their evil attempts will backfire, the weapons they use will be faulty!"

❝ We're told that there's a difference between the blameless and the wicked and their futures. ❞

It can be stressful when we feel under attack. However, God wants us to have the attitude of the Road Runner. He knows that his enemy is going to try to attack him. He also knows that his enemy is going to fail. Trusting God is having a confidence like this. We can go about our business secure in the fact that the lies of our attackers will not succeed. In the heat of the challenge, it's the enemy that will wilt like a flower without water, with no one to renew their strength. This is why we're encouraged not to be worrying about what plan they may be devising. It'll backfire on them and they'll wish they hadn't started it. Their influence will fade. A better investment of our time and energy is put to use by discovering more of God when we pray. Take time to thank God for who He is and what He's like. If you're not sure of what He's like, read through a Psalm and think deeply on it. As you do this your connection with God will grow, as will your confidence in God's promise that He will help you. Wait patiently for God to come through for you! This is one of the ways that you can build the house of your life upon the rock that is Jesus.

PRAY

Lord God Almighty. You are my caring Father God. I want to know what you are like today. Lead me to know You more. In Jesus' name.

Day 19

THE LORD'S
enemies
ARE LIKE
the flowers
OF THE FIELD,
they will
BE CONSUMED

TAKERS AND GIVERS
Day 20

The wicked borrow and do not repay,
but the righteous give generously;

A while back we had a pool tournament. The idea was simple. Every person hands over 50 pence to join the competition. All the 50ps get put in a pot and the winner takes all. Though it sounds harsh, the rule is: No pay, no play. Of course, that doesn't stop people from begging to enter the tournament without money, promising to pay the 50 pence next time they attend! Such people (after being knocked out in the first round) conveniently forget to pay their 50p debt the next time they visit; yet if they had won the competition, they would have expected to claim their winnings! Yes of course I've had people do this! Sometimes we have to be generous to others at the risk of being let down!

It's easy to observe the poor standards of those around us and be tempted to do the same. "If they can get away with it, why can't I?" We might say. However, God's way of doing things is totally different, loving those we would rather hate, forgiving those who have done us wrong, acting out of generosity rather than harbouring bitterness. This is the trusting and doing good we read about in verse 3, knowing that now we are God's children, we behave differently from our natural instincts. Instead, we live out our true identity: as sons and daughters of God's kingdom. We are called by God to live out our lives in goodness and truthfulness. This isn't easy. In a world where we are told we have rights and to look after number one, putting others first can seem a bit unnecessary. Yet as God's people, we are given access to everything we need to love others, even those who hate us. This doesn't mean that we just stand aside and let evil have its way. It does mean that we change our attitude to understand those we don't get on with, rather than labelling them as evil.

It can be tempting to judge others according to the good moral standards that God wants for our own lives. Maybe you've seen online or heard about someone who is known to be a Christian who has done something they shouldn't have. It's easy for us to turn against that person and negatively label them. However, God wants us to be generous in the way that we view others. Remember when Jesus said to pray, it is to forgive others of their wrongs against us, in the same way He has forgiven us (Matt 6:12-14). Jesus also said "Give and it will be given to you, a good measure, pressed down, shaken together and running over, will be poured into your lap." He was talking here about not judging others. The amount we use to judge other people, is the same which God will use to judge you and me. Check it out! It's in Luke 6:37-38. So be generous! Especially when you are tempted to judge another person.

❝ God wants us to be generous in the way that we view others. ❞

How quick are you to judge others? Do you ever try and put yourself in their shoes and wonder if their actions are more innocent than it first seems? Do you forgive, rather than hold a grudge? If we want

93

God to give us the benefit of the doubt when we mess up, we ought to do the same for others. God is very generous to us and doesn't treat us as our wrongdoings deserve.

So we are to live by a different standard. It's a standard of righteousness which pleases God. At times this might be at odds with what we feel is just or fair. Why should so and so get away with what they have done?? I say let our first instinct be one that is generous to others, rather than judging them guilty. Otherwise we might just be condemning someone whom God has given a second chance. We know how many second chances He has given us! As we have read, God will deal with the wicked in His way and in His perfect timing.

PRAY

Father God. I ask that You would help me to be generous in my thoughts and actions to those who I think don't deserve it. Help me to hold back from judging others. Instead help me to see these people as You see them. I know You have always been generous to me. Thank You!

Day 20

PRAYER SPACE — FORGIVING OTHERS

To forgive is to release the hard feelings you feel toward a person, so that if you were to think of them, you would not have hate, bitterness or rage towards them.

You might say:
> "But it wasn't fair what they did" or "it was not right"
> "How can I forgive? They do not deserve it."

• Forgiving someone doesn't mean what they did to you was right.
• Forgiving does not mean that they "get off free." If it is a crime they have committed, they still have to answer to the law and to God.
• Forgiveness does not mean you give up all your rights, or that you have to allow that person back into your life.
• Forgiving someone does not mean you have to forget what they did.

If you decide not to forgive someone:
• It doesn't hurt the person who harmed you like you might think!
• It actually hurts only you
• It places you in emotional chains and will torment you
• It may cause you to grow bitter, angry and change you in a negative way
• It blocks the fullness of God in your life

Forgiving those who hurt you:
• Means you can step aside to let God deal with that person
• Will remove a heavy emotional burden from you
• Sets you free
• It closes a door which allows the enemy to have access to you

Forgiving allows you to say:
> "I choose to forgive even though they may not deserve it"
> "I choose to let this person go into God's hands"
> "I am not going to be their judge"

Take a look at these Bible verses before we pray:

Matthew 6:14-15

"For if you forgive others the wrongs they have done to you, your Father in heaven will also forgive you. But if you do not forgive others, then your Father will not forgive the wrongs you have done."

Read Matthew 18:21-35

Then Peter came to Jesus and asked, "Lord, how many times shall I forgive my brother or sister who sins against me? Up to seven times?" Jesus answered, "I tell you, not seven times, but seventy times seven. "Therefore, the kingdom of heaven is like a king who wanted to settle accounts with his servants. (See Matt 18:21-35).

"This is how my heavenly Father will treat each of you unless you forgive your brother or sister from your heart."

Luke 6:37

"Do not judge others, and God will not judge you; do not condemn others, and God will not condemn you; forgive others and God will forgive you.

Forgiving others is a choice we make and not an emotional feeling
Forgiving will set you free

Father God. I now understand how important forgiving those who have hurt me is, and how not forgiving others actually hurts me even more. I want to forgive, so please come close as I need your help to say these words:

Lord Jesus, I choose to forgive _____ (say their name) for _____ (tell Jesus what they did to you). I release to you all the hard feelings that I have toward this person. Please remove every chain that is holding me back from receiving the freedom that you want me to enjoy. Please transform me by your power to live out this forgiveness today, tomorrow and every day. In your powerful name Jesus!

BLESSINGS AND CURSES
Day 21

those the LORD blesses will inherit the land,
but those he curses will be destroyed.

Some time ago, I found myself in a Catholic monastery. The place was vast, a real maze of corridors, stairwells and rooms. Finally, I managed to locate the lobby to make my exit, when a lady approached me and asked where she could go to get a blessing. This got me thinking... A blessing from God is a very noble thing to be looking for, don't you think? Maybe you've heard it said in a prayer for God to bless someone, or you might recognise the word from the song "The Blessing;" but what actually is a blessing?

There's a story in the book of Genesis (chapter 27) where a man called Jacob is determined to get his dad's best blessing ahead of his older twin. In those days the father's best blessing was reserved for the first-born son. It was given towards the end of the father's life and was a bit like telling his son about the inheritance he would receive. Almost like a prayer over the life of each of his children, the father would declare the good things that he believed God had in store for them. Naturally Jacob was thrilled as his dad spoke good things about his future, talking of an abundance of riches, the position of leadership and power that would lead to his success.

97

These were God's words spoken through Isaac for Jacob; therefore God would certainly make them happen.

In Old Testament times, there was nothing more important than having God's blessing. This word blessing is not just good wishes, like the nice words that you might read in a birthday card, but rather they are a prophetic declaration. These are words that have the power of God behind them that will come to pass. When we read the words of verse 22 "...those the Lord blesses will inherit the land," it's about the good things that God has prepared for you. Maybe you need protection from harm? Or you have a physical illness that needs to be fixed? It could be you are talented at something and you hope that God will make you successful in your field of expertise? Perhaps you just know that all good things come from God and you want his favour and good fortune to be working for you in your everyday living? These are all blessings that the Lord has for us and He doesn't mind us seeking Him out for these things.

Some people say that we shouldn't seek God for His gifts, but as we see in the life of Jacob, God rewarded his determination as he sought to secure God's blessing. God wants us to ask for His help and His favour. We're told that those who are His children, who delight in God, will "inherit the land." So, does God actually have a plot of ground set aside for me? Umm... This phrase is an amazing piece of picture language referring back to a time when God did actually reserve land for His people. In the Old Testament, after the Israelites were led out of slavery from Egypt, God's plan was to secure a place for them to live as free people. The land they were going to was a place "flowing with milk and honey;" a home where they would have all they needed and where God would generously provide for them. That is what they needed at that time and God promises to give us what we need today and tomorrow.

> **"** We see in the life of Jacob, God rewarded his determination as he sought to secure God's blessing. **"**

There is however, another contrast in the verse we read. We have previously seen that the blameless are under God's care, but those intent on harming God's people will not go unpunished. Those God curses will be destroyed, cut off from God's blessings. Knowing God, is not just joining His team and then living however we want. The blameless are those who genuinely follow Jesus, put Him first and live their lives in obedience to His teaching. When we hand over our past, present and future to Jesus to do with what He wants, we will experience His immense blessing as we let Him into every area of our lives.

PRAY

Father God. Thank You that You have good things in store for me every day. I trust You with my life and my future. In Jesus' name.

Day 21

PRAYER SPACE

Below is something called a word cloud. Why not turn up Psalm 46 and have a think about what God is like. Then just write the words or phrases down as they come to mind, big or small horizontal or vertical on the opposite page...

BEGINNING

His words are true

The Living God

KING OF KINGS

FATHER

Defender

Guide

THE RESURRECTED KING

compassionate

HE IS

FAITHFUL

MAJESTIC

everlasting

Longing with love for us

The resurrection and the life

Provider

INCREDIBLE

Tireless in His pursuit of us

GRACIOUS

Worthy of the Highest praise

WORTHY

ABOUNDING IN LOVE

The **ALMIGHTY**

full of love

NEVER FAILING

My inspiration

The Lamb who takes away the sins of the world

THE END

STEPPING CONFIDENTLY
Day 22

The LORD makes firm the steps
of the one who delights in him;

Ever thought of having a go at Parkour? Also known as free running, it's a kind of extreme sport that sees participants summersaulting over barriers, clinging onto ledges and jumping off rooftops, before landing in a kind of forward roll and running off. It looks impressive, scary and dangerous. There are plenty of examples of this sport (or is it art?) on YouTube, with some incredible sequences filmed in well-known locations such as London and Paris. However, jumping from one rooftop apartment to another over the width of street isn't something you just decide to do and take your chances. To the untrained eye it looks easy and unplanned, like the natural skills of jungle creatures swinging from tree to tree. It is however, the very opposite. Parkour requires a lot of preparation, with careful planning and practice needed. Before filming a sequence, every jump and swing is thought out ahead of time, with each step paced out and decided upon beforehand to ensure unnecessary risks aren't taken. If not properly checked, a loose roof tile or slippery drain pipe could land runners in a fails video montage, with the ambulance journey edited out!

The bit that we read today talks about how God carefully plans the way to the opportunities that He knows will delight your heart and fulfil His purposes for your life. His plan for your life is not some last-minute, thrown together idea, written down hastily on a scrap of paper. No. God, with great forethought and care causes multiple situations to come together in order for it all to take place. I remember when getting engaged to Debs, we secretly asked God to confirm whether He wanted us to be married. That week we were at a big Christian event and during one of the main stage events, we turned around to see a group holding up a banner with the words "For Pete's sake marry me!!" on it. Neither Debs nor I had anything to do with organising the banner, so we took it that God had instigated it and were married a year later. Think of the timing and planning that would have been needed to have made that happen. Just days after we had asked for God's confirmation, in a venue with thousands of people, to be situated so we could see the words that a group of girls unknown to us had randomly taken the time to create for a guy named Pete!

" His plan for your life is not some last-minute, thrown together idea, written down hastily on a scrap of paper. **"**

Sometimes we take on way too much responsibility for the decisions we have to make in life, when God is like "I have this covered. Just follow me and it will all fall into place." When we submit our lives to God and involve Him in our decision-making process, we need not stress if we are getting it wrong. God sees our future steps and the outcomes of certain decisions. Like a multiverse of possibilities, He can tell what is best for us and the consequences of our decisions.

God helps those who delight in Him with the choices of our lives. He ensures that we will be presented with the opportunities that will benefit us, as well as the wisdom to know what to do. This is in contrast to those who do evil. God brings security to our life circumstances when we put Him first. When we read the words "the Lord makes firm the steps of the one who delights in Him," we're given this picture of someone making their way on a journey, possibly over uneven ground, facing new and difficult challenges, through the different stages of life.

Maybe you're wondering about your future and how to get where you want to be. With God we can take confident steps into the wider world, knowing that He is influencing everything around us to be in-sync with His plans. He can take away the worry and replace it with wisdom which brings success. He'll also open doors for you that he will close for others! He says "I will bless those who delight in me!"

PRAY

Father God. Thank You that You love to favourably influence my future for my good, according to Your purposes. Do what You want to with my life. I trust You with my life. I refuse to believe any fears that make me think negatively about my future. You are my firm foundation and I know that You have good things in store for me. Thank You. In Jesus' name!

Day 22

THE LORD
makes firm
THE STEPS
of the one who
DELIGHTS
in him;

AVOIDING CALAMITY
Day 23

though he may stumble, he will not fall,
*for the L*ORD* upholds him with his hand.*

Have you made any big mistakes recently? I really hate making mistakes, but the truth is when we're learning something new, we get stuff wrong. In life we're learning all the time. It's okay, it's part of being human. I've made plenty of mistakes. I remember when I was in training as a youth worker, we had a small group meeting in someone's house. Towards the end of the session a couple who attended the church knocked on the door and brought in some boys whom they had just met and lived locally. We started to chat with the lads to get to know them. However, things got a bit awkward and cringey and when the man who had brought them in started laying his hand on each of the boy's shoulders and saying "The Lord bless you. And the Lord bless you." I have no idea what the lads thought, but they were out pretty quick and then the couple left. When the couple had gone, I said "I dunno about you, but that couple were really weird!" At which point one of the young people said "That's my dad!"

It's easy to feel like a failure when you make a mistake. When we fail it can appear like there's no going back to the way things were.

However, what we read today is that God is with us and will help us when we've messed it up. Waking up the day after we've failed big time can be tough, but we have a promise here that it is not the end. Instead, it can be a beginning. Sometimes in our efforts to achieve our ambitions we try to do too much too quickly. Maybe we have high expectations of what we need to achieve, or how we should be coping in a situation. If we are not meeting those expectations, we feel like a failure; but the good news is that God is so good at turning failure into success! Just read the Bible and see the amount of people who failed God and are counted as heroes today.

> **"** Waking up the day after we've failed big time can be tough, but we have a promise here that it is not the end. **"**

We just read that God holds on to us with His hand to prevent disaster from ruining our lives when we mess up. You know when you're running, chasing after a ball and you fall forward because your legs aren't going as fast as your body? We're reading picture language of someone who is stumbling and about to fall headlong into calamity. The promise is that God will be close by, to prevent the fall in our worst moments. Did you know that God's definition of success is different from the human view? You don't have to be top of the class, given a prize, be on TV, earn celebrity status, or accumulate lots of money to be successful. I believe God values faithfulness as a much better measure of success than achievement. You can achieve greatness in God's eyes without ever coming in first place. Jesus has some important words in the book of Revelation to the followers of Jesus, "hold fast" (Rev 3:11). Following Him faithfully and with a whole heart will lead us to achieve the successes God has for us. Stick with Him. Don't let go! Failing ourselves, others or God is not the end. The enemy wants you to give up, but the Lord wants you to keep going. He will turn what the enemy meant for evil into something truly wonderful. The fact is that we will all fail.

At this point, you might be asking, but how could this happen to me? I thought God was making a way for my steps. Yes He is! Just remember, we're not robots. We have free will to live in partnership with God. He gives us everything we need to guide us, as well as allowing us the freedom to choose faithfulness. There is also an enemy who will lie to us, trick us and confuse us in an attempt to lead us away from a life of faithfulness to God. This life is not an easy one! Yet God promises to be faithful to us and to support us when we stumble in life and need a helping hand. Sometimes we think failure only leads to calamity; but in God's book it leads to greater opportunities than we could ever have accomplished. The opportunities God creates for us are ones that bring a success that we could never have achieved on our own!

PRAY

Father God. I realise that my life exists to bring You glory. Thank You that You turn the bad stuff into something better than I could ever imagine!

Day 23

XP
Day 24

I was young and now I am old,
yet I have never seen the righteous forsaken
or their children begging bread.

Let's talk about XP. If you're ever going to get on in the gaming world, you'll know that XP is a component that is helpful to your success. What is XP? It's short for experience points which can be earned if you do the right stuff as you progress through the game. For example, in Minecraft, the moment you extract coal, you'll be given XP. Lots of experience points will be handy later for accessing more advanced tasks that give your weapons and tools a greater versatility. An upgraded weapon will require less hits to smite a skeleton. This will get you to the treasure he is protecting quicker than his arrows can send you back to the respawn point. XP on Rocket League helps you to move up levels unlocking reward items to customise your vehicles with fancy new rims or a goal explosion that makes your opponents look on in awe. The levelling up brought by experience points also enables you to contend against better online opponents, enhancing your own skills along the way. This in turn will improve your ability to progress through the game more effectively. In a nutshell, having a high XP score normally means that you are an expert in the game and should have your own YouTube channel to make your wisdom known to the masses!

Such wisdom only comes through experience. Someone new to the game may have mad skills, but knowledge to get to the really cool stuff of the game only comes through hours of play. Experience is knowing how to deal with a situation because you have encountered something like it in the game before. This is what gives you the edge. Knowledge if used in the right way can lead to greater wisdom. It's easy to picture Yoda from Star Wars saying the words in the bit we read today, "Old am I now, young was I." What we read today gives us clues to the backdrop of the entire Psalm 37. Everything we have read (and will read) in this Psalm is the divinely inspired words of a godly old man. Possibly the reflections of King David, he is giving us insight into the ways that God works in the lives of His people. What better person to write, than one who has been through it all and seen good outcomes again and again of those who live the life of faith! You see, it's quite easy to mistakenly view things from a short-term perspective, where we see the bad stuff going on around us and think that nothing is happening to stop it. We can assume that what we're going through is going to result in the the worst possible outcome and that God has lost interest in us. It's easy to think the worst and to consider giving up.

The encouragement today is "Don't give up when things go wrong, it's not the end." God does not forsake His children. This is the truth coming from someone looking back with many years of XP in this journey of life. He observes God working in the now, where our needs are more immediate, as well as in the long-term where we might have to wait for solutions. Because God sees our beginning from our end, His time scale might be a bit different from ours. These are the wise words of someone who has been through the difficult levels of life in the best and worst of times. Here, patience has been learned and a confidence in God has been built by seeing God at work over the years. Sometimes we wonder if God is doing anything after just one week! Often God does work His wonders in a short space of time, but He also works His wonders over months, years and decades.

> **"** Because God sees our beginning from our end, His time scale might be a bit different from ours. **"**

What if you are desperate for God to answer a really important prayer? As a slightly younger "old man," I can tell you that I have been in this situation more than once. Don't be fearful that God will take too long. His timing is perfect. Wait patiently, keep praying! Fight your battles in prayer if you want your actions to help, rather than hinder your cause. Keep talking to God and involve Him in every detail of what you are going through. God is with you and will help you! If you want to take this deeper with God now, there's a prayer space over the page to help you to do this.

PRAY

Father God. I have chosen to trust You with my life. Thank you that You are at work and that You have already gone before me. In Jesus' name!

Day 24

PRAYER SPACE

BLESS BLESS BLESS
Day 25

They are always generous and lend freely;
their children will be a blessing.

How does generosity make you feel? Say you're out shopping with a friend and they say "Let me pay for this" when you stop at a milkshake bar. Or you've forgotten your bus pass and a friend pays for your ticket. Do you feel cared for and looked after? Maybe it makes you feel valued, honoured or loved? The impact of our kind actions on other people are greater than we think. Even small acts of kindness, like taking the time to make a card of appreciation for someone, shows generosity and can have a lasting effect.

We've already looked in previous devotions at how God blesses us. As His children God also loves to see us acting in a similar way, loving others because it's the way He does things. Sometimes we can be the person that God uses to bless others. You don't have to be a millionaire to be generous to someone else. The kind of thinking that says "When I'm rich I'll help others," misunderstands how God works. You see, when we give others what God has given to us, He multiplies it, giving it the potential to do great amounts of good. Every time that we are generous to others, we are showing people what

114

God is like. This is what being righteous is, it's living in the goodness of God in a way that blesses others.

Jesus always led by this example, so that we could see what it looks like in practice. He said, "Freely you have received; freely give" (Matt 10:8). You and I have received the favour of God simply by accepting it and He wants us to pass this on freely to others. His kingdom works much like the way Jesus gave thanks and passed out five loaves and two fishes to the disciples (Matt 14:16-21). The more the disciples gave out, the more loaves and fish they had to give away! God's supply does not run out. His is a rich supply. If anything, the limits to it are only the ones we put on it. There is so much that He wants to give if we will be open to it!

> **" The kind of thinking that says "When I'm rich I'll help others," misunderstands how God works. "**

At this point you might be thinking. "Oh man. I have to do more for God." Hey wait a minute. Think of an apple tree. Is it busy trying hard to do better? Do you see it straining to produce fruit? I'm not sure the fruit would appeal to me in the same way if I'm honest! Remember the disciples gave from what Jesus gave them. If they hadn't been hanging out with Jesus, they'd not have had anything to give to others. What has God given you that He wants you to be generous with? Is it your money? Or your time? Could it be doing something you are good at? What opportunities to be generous is God leading you into? Maybe it's as simple as being generous with kindness, using our words to encourage someone at home or school. It could be giving up time to do things that help others, or even helping in your local church or youth group.

Being with Jesus energises and changes us. He gives the Holy Spirit and His power to make our generosity go further than we could possibly imagine. To try and do all the things mentioned above without taking time to talk with and connect with Jesus would be possible, but will likely wear you out. Like a tree that produces apples it will produce more fruit in good soil, so as we connect with the goodness of Jesus, we find we naturally want to bless others with what He gives us. Our character will grow in love and confidence to be generous to others because of His power within us. Instead of a selfish outlook, we become more loving and caring towards others. It's a natural transformation that gradually takes place from spending time with Jesus.

PRAY

Father God, give me a generous heart. Thank You for all that You have given me. Inspire me to see what good things I have that will bless others. May my words encourage, strengthen and comfort others today. I want all that I do to honour You and show Your generosity to others. In Jesus' name.

Day 25

they are always

GENEROUS

and lend freely;

THEIR CHILDREN WILL

be a blessing

ORIENTATION SKILLS
Day 26

Turn from evil and do good;
then you will dwell in the land forever.

Have you ever been travelling on a boat and started to feel a bit queasy? It's hard when you're worried about being sick to think of anything else. The weird thing about seasickness is that it's not a virus or tummy bug that will send you rushing off to the toilet, but rather the brain which is causing the issue. When seasickness hits, your brain is having trouble with the messages sent to it by the balancing system in your inner ear. Is there a way to stop seasickness? You'll be pleased to know that there are things that can be done to ease it.

First what you need to do is to reorientate yourself on the boat. Go get some fresh air, drink some water to rehydrate and face the direction where the boat is headed. Advice online also suggests taking the driving seat, but if you aren't qualified (or authorised) to pilot a boat, the next best thing is to keep your eyes on the horizon. These changes can help make all the difference, especially if you have a long journey ahead!

Why the seasickness instruction? The advice that I have just given you for preventing seasickness, also works when we get anxious or stressed. Sometimes the enemy can attack our thinking and cause us to feel overwhelmed and our brain has trouble coping with it. This can happen in the most ordinary of everyday situations. It could be a crowded space that sets off something in your brain and you suddenly feel uncomfortable and needing some room to breathe. Or you're dreading a particular moment coming up in your day and so your mind starts stressing about how it's going to turn out. When the brain is stuck trying to process something, it's easy to feel overwhelmed. Much like seasickness, times like these can't just be ignored; it can be a very real problem, with real consequences.

What then do you do? If it feels like you are starting to feel anxious, altering your physical space by getting some air and hydration is a good idea. Much like being on the boat, you need to reorientate what you are focusing on. We read the words today, "turn from evil." This is all about turning away from the rut of negative thinking that is attacking us. Did you know that spending time with God can give us the power to control our thinking? Yes, self-control is a fruit of the Spirit, where God gives us His supernatural ability, when in our own power it would be impossible. Much like being on that boat and feeling seasick, we can reorientate our thinking to stop looking at what is bad and evil and instead to focus on what is good.

> **"** Self-control is a fruit of the Spirit, where God gives us His supernatural ability, when in our own power it would be impossible. **"**

Instead of fearing the worst, you have the power to take control and start to think about the good things that are around you. Maybe you have a friend close by who is giving you support. Remind yourself of the good things that God is doing in your life. In your mind, begin to thank Him for them. This is just like facing the direction that you are headed in the boat. Take some time to think about the things you have thanked God for and consider how these have come about. See how God has been (and is) working in your life.

Next, develop your thinking further by focusing your thoughts on the horizon, that is: God and who He is. You have noticed where He is at work. Now what do you notice about God and his character? Tell God what you love about Him. Thank Him for how He is good at turning bad situations into really good ones! Ask the Holy Spirit to come close and show you more of Jesus and the Father. Give God control of everything that happens next, both the minutes that follow and your longer-term needs. God wants to help you to turn from fear, refusing to believe the lies of fear will do you a lot of good. When you feel you can, reach out to others who can help you.[2] We can't do this life alone, facing in the right direction is the first step to a longer process of restoration which is the inheritance that God has for you.

PRAY

Father God. Thank You that You don't leave me when I am stressed, but You are right there with me. Help me to notice You more! In Jesus' name.

Day 26

PRAYER SPACE

Be still and know
that I am God

Psalm 46:10

WAITING FOR JUSTICE
Day 27

*For the L*ORD *loves the just
and will not forsake his faithful ones.
Wrongdoers will be completely destroyed;
the offspring of the wicked will perish.*

It was a very sad and shocking day when we learned of the news that Russia had invaded the country of Ukraine. The attack was unprovoked. Russia had first said that the 100,000 Russian troops who were stationed at Ukraine's border, weren't going to attack the country, instead they were just doing training exercises; but still they attacked. What was worse, were the reports of the 40-mile-long military convoy of tanks approaching the Ukrainian capital. The Ukrainians were determined to fight to the last man to stop them, but on paper, the odds were very much against them. However, the Ukrainians have this in their favour, they have justice on their side.

We read today that the Lord "will not forsake his faithful ones." As I write this, the story isn't over in what has become a war. With threats from Russia of nuclear action to any outside countries who come to Ukraine's aid, the situation is desperate. Yet what we thought would be certain doom for the Ukraine capital city, has not happened. The Ukrainian army, assisted by many volunteers are putting up a surprising fight against this military superpower. The 40-mile Russian convoy never made it through. Many of its armoured vehicles have been destroyed, with others turning back the way they came. Today the battle still rages. The Russians have caused much destruction to the country and its people. The Ukrainian church is praying. We are all praying as we hear the heart-breaking stories of families separated, innocents killed and atrocities too horrible to mention taking place.

You know, before the victory, when the challenge is at its worst, there is the temptation to turn away from hoping in the Lord. It was like this for the Hebrews, when they were being mistreated in Egypt. Moses was a baby when the Egyptians began to harm the Hebrews. As a man, Moses returned after many years and the Lord used him to set the Hebrew slaves free. David, the writer of this Psalm encountered many wars and battles. He suffered defeat and loss and challenging times, as well as being victorious over his enemies. Yet his words from the Lord are that God does not leave his people. Sometimes there is a time of extreme hardship to endure, before the promises of God are fulfilled with justice being done.

When stuff like this happens, a big question which we can ask is "Does God not care about the unjust way bullies carry on?" We're told here that God won't abandon those badly treated, because he loves justice. He actually hates evil done to others. It makes him so angry!! We know that this world is messed up because of selfishness, greed and hate. If we were to trace back the actions of the Russian President Vladimir Putin and detect the thought process which led to his act of war, we would see selfishness at the heart of it all.

❝Sometimes there is a time of extreme hardship to endure, before the promises of God are fulfilled with justice being done.❞

The good news is that God favours the just, because justice is in His nature. God acts on behalf of the innocent and the weak. Do you have a just cause that you need help with? Trust Him, because His favour is with you. As you live out this trust by faithfully staying connected with Jesus, taking in His words and believing His promises, He will be with you in the difficulty. You will actually be partnering with God against those wrongfully treating you. The Lord is working out a bright future for you.

PRAY

Father God. Thank You that You have good things in store for me. I put my trust in You. I know that this means doing things Your way. Give me the wisdom I need, so that I will see Your solutions working out in the difficulties I face. In Jesus' name.

Day 27

for the lord loves

THE JUST

and will not forsake his faithful ones.

WRONGDOERS WILL

be completely destroyed;

THE OFFSPRING

of the wicked will perish.

THE EVERLASTING PROMISE
Day 28

The righteous will inherit the land and dwell in it forever.

After reigning for 70 years as Queen of the United Kingdom, Elizabeth II died. The time of mourning following the Queen's death saw around 250,000 people visit the Palace of Westminster to pay their respects, queueing for up to 14 hours to give thanks for her life. This was a heartfelt response, recognising the servant-hearted, righteous nature of one who lived a sacrificial life of duty for her country. Those who visited her coffin lying in state, spoke of how she had always been there, always present, providing a reassuring constancy to her loyal subjects. She was active in guiding Prime Ministers with wise advice, handing out awards to honour people's faithful service, with messages to the people in the form of an annual Christmas speech. But now she is gone. She will very much be missed.

Did you know that she believed in God? Hers was a living faith in the life death and resurrection of Jesus Christ. She lived it out every day. Her seat on earth's throne is now empty, but now she has a seat in heaven. She is with Jesus in paradise. We've read today that "The righteous will inherit the land and dwell in it forever." This is more than the promise of an earthly inheritance, but of a life with God that stretches into eternity. This life is not all there is. It's easy to lose sight of the future, of what is to come, when we're worried about the present. Questions can come into our minds, asking "Where is God?" or "Why isn't God doing anything now?" Of course, God is working both in our present, and also in our futures. The inheritance that God gives to His people begins from the moment we accept Him and commit to follow Him. It will continue uninterrupted through death into the afterlife.

Let's consider this "future glory" which the Bible tells us about, where after death, those who know Jesus will be with Him. All crying and pain and trouble will be ended. We'll live in the presence of God as His people forever. Death and loss will be forgotten; and when Jesus returns, all things will be made new. One significant difference with our existence today, is that we'll be in a place where the devil is not and thus evil will not be there either. How is all this possible? How can we live in a world without evil? From the beginning of time, God has been working on our behalf, so that our inheritance would enable us to have this life and be with Him forever. God knew that the presence of sin in our own hearts would always form a barrier between humankind and God. Human effort would never reach the standards required to overcome that barrier. So God chose to live as a human and give His very life to do what we couldn't do. This is the gospel that Jesus came to offer all of humankind and which is only received by accepting and following Jesus, the one whom God sent.

❝ We'll live in the presence of God as His people forever. ❞

If all crying and pain will one day be ended in the future, does that mean we have to live with it now? Jesus did say that in this life we will have trouble (John 16:33). Jesus also demonstrated by His life that He wants us to enjoy heaven's blessings before we die. After all, He did say that we could ask God for His will and kingdom to take place on this earth as it does in heaven (Matt 6:10). What is it like in heaven? There's nothing bad! People have been made well, they are happy and joyful! God is powerfully present with His people. We will see Jesus's face to face! So today, we can pray for the good things of God to become a reality in our world. God sent the Holy Spirit after Jesus had gone up to heaven so that we would experience how real God really is! He loves to communicate with us, to teach us and remind us of what He is like in so many ways so that we can have a glimpse of what it will be like when we enter into our eternal inheritance.

PRAY

Father God. Thank You for the heavenly inheritance that You have in store for me. Teach me how to access heaven's blessings on this earth. The way You work is amazing! Show me how to partner with You. In Jesus' name!

Day 28

GOOD ADVICE
Day 29

*The mouths of the righteous utter wisdom,
and their tongues speak what is just.*

What is wisdom? Let me start by giving you an example of what wisdom is not. This is a story from "The book of heroic failures":

Intending to steal cash from a supermarket in 1977, a Southampton thief employed a unique tactic to divert the till girl's attention. His method was to collect a trolley full of goods, arrive at her till and put down £10 by way of payment. She would then take the money and open the till, upon which he would snatch its cash.

He arrived at the cash desk and put down the £10. She took it and opened the till; but there was only £4.37 in it. Undeterred, the Southampton thief snatched the money and made his getaway, having lost £5.63 on the raid. The till girl was considerably uncertain what to do for the best. She screamed briefly until calmed by her friend Betty.

Yes. That was all kinds of stupid. Of course, we don't know what he was thinking, but by ignoring God's moral standard on stealing and justice, he risked his own short-term freedom if caught and his long-term ability to get future employment. That's without considering why his target was just a humble supermarket, rather than a high value jewellery store!

Wisdom begins with God. When we read and take in God's words as found in the Bible, we can find we are shielded from a lot of bother. By following the commandment "Don't steal," we are first demonstrating God's love, by treating others as we would want to be treated. It's a wise course of action because it protects us from all sorts of trouble, be it a bad reputation, prison or a criminal record. There is also wisdom in obeying the command not to steal, because it makes a way for God to provide for our needs. Catch this for a moment. Sometimes the temptation is to go about things in a way that disregards God's moral standards, to use lies or deception to get what we want. However, following God's way when we need something (resisting the urge to use ungodly tactics) can lead to God providing for us. This is where faith comes into play. Can we show that we trust God even when it hurts to do the right thing? This is the wisest course of action.

❝When we read and take in God's words as found in the Bible, we can find we are shielded from a lot of bother.❞

The idea of wisdom here, is someone who humbly submits themselves to God's rule over their lives. They seek out His thoughts and process them in their minds to understand God better. The Holy Spirit is also known as the "Spirit of wisdom." Spending time with Him will give you wisdom that you could never have gained on your own. As we have seen in previous devotions this can come with age and experience, but the Holy Spirit will also inspire us with wisdom when we have invested the time to discover what He thinks.

We read today that the "mouths of the righteous utter wisdom." Wisdom is one of the most amazing gifts someone can have. Maybe you want to be a good friend. God can give you wise insight to help resolve that tough relationship that your friend is going through. Wouldn't it be incredible to know exactly what to say or do to help them sort it out? Just remember, God's wisdom goes hand in hand with His good moral standards and justice. You may have the wise solution for your friend, but it's another thing whether they listen to you or not! Today we read that those who hang out with God will naturally have wise advice. The best givers of godly wisdom are those who are kind and loving with their advice, not arrogant know-it-alls with something to prove.

PRAY

Father God. Thank You that You are the wisest being there is. You are also the most humble. As I seek Your wisdom, cause me to be more like You. May the words of my mouth and the thoughts of my heart be pleasing to You.

Day 29

PRAYER SPACE

On the page opposite are different starting points for talking to God.

Perhaps you feel inspired to write a poem, or simply to sing a song you know. There's space on both pages to write or draw around the pictures as you feel inspired to. Sometimes I just listen to a song and start drawing shapes as I consider God and Him being close to me. Often the results are surprising! Why not give it a try?!

May my meditation on Your words

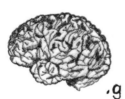

.g to You

What is it that You are saying to me?

It's Your breath in my lungs

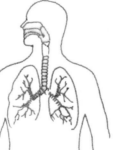

So I'll pour out my praise to You

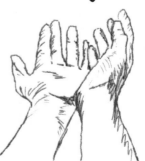

I'll bring You more than a song

What can I give

Lord I give You my heart

to You my King?

133

BREAKING THE RULES?
Day 30

The law of their God is in their hearts;
their feet do not slip.

During the Coronavirus pandemic the UK Prime Minister Boris Johnson got himself in a whole heap of trouble, by setting laws that he didn't follow. As the Prime Minister, he appeared during special broadcasts on TV to tell the nation the rules we were to stick to, so that the spread of the Covid-19 virus could be controlled. When things were pretty bad, we were not allowed to meet in youth groups, instead we went online, using the video call app Zoom. People had to wear masks, to stay 2 metres apart and not go into each other's houses and definitely not have any parties!

Yet when Christmastime came around, Boris and his co-workers messed up. This was all kept secret until months later, when someone spilled the beans and reported that the Prime Minister had appeared at a number of gatherings, some with cheese and wine! Understandably, people were upset. "Why were we having to pass on attending important gatherings, such as funerals and weddings, when Boris wasn't keeping to his own rules?" they demanded. It appears that Boris knew the laws in his mind, but had not taken their seriousness to heart.

134

We're reading more today about the people of God, known as "the righteous." This is a name tag for those who are faithful in their devotion of God. The righteous take time to discover what pleases God so that they can follow His ways. As we saw yesterday, God's words bring about a wisdom that avoids the potential pitfalls of life. Maybe there are some days when you find yourself slipping up when it comes to doing things you know you shouldn't? Perhaps you've thought "How can I stop doing these things that I know are wrong ??" Listen, we are all human, no one is perfect; but we are given a clue as to what sets the righteous apart, so as not to turn our backs on God. We're told that the righteous don't fall into faithlessness because "the law of God is in their hearts."

The heart describes an unseen part of our lives. It's that deep place within us which drives our desires and emotions. With our heart we feel love, drawing us to someone, making them feel special to us. Love can be a powerful motivating force to give us the will to ask someone out on a date. When our heart desires something or someone, we'll do anything for them. Maybe you've been faced with a choice where your heart wants something that makes no sense to your head?

The idea of storing something in your heart is like hiding something away, as a something to be treasured, because it is loved. It goes beyond reading, like a memory verse to be recited at a moment's notice. It's more than having an understanding for God's words, so that we know what they mean. When we have stored God's word in our hearts, our everyday decisions and actions reflect God and His words. His words have become the culture and identity of our lives. Therefore, our natural tendencies to bad attitudes or behaviours are overwritten by God's words, transforming us to live God's way rather than our own. In Jesus' day, many of the religious leaders had only stored God's words in their minds. They followed all of God's commands, but their uncaring attitudes towards others revealed that they did not know God Himself. Jesus said of them! "These people honour me with their lips, but their hearts are far from me" (Matthew 15:8).

❝When we have stored God's word in our hearts, our everyday decisions and actions reflect God and His words.❞

The heart is where our motivation comes from. When you read God's words with an expectation and desire to discover something of God, you are opening that treasure box, ready to store something new. With this attitude, you will surely meet with God, hear from Him and learn about how to live daily in partnership with Him.

PRAY

Father God. Thank You that Your words do me good when I take them to heart. I want to follow your ways. Holy Spirit, please inspire my heart to understand and receive what You have for me. In Jesus' name.

Day 30

PRAYER SPACE — HOW TO PRAY

PRAYING IS DEVELOPED
- It starts with a word
- It grows into a relationship

PRAYING IS A RELATIONSHIP
- Tell Him your thoughts and heart stuff
- Find out more about Him

PRAYING IS A PLACE OF GROWTH IN GOD
- The Spirit of God works in you
- Your life will change for the better

HANDY TIPS
Have a listen to a Christian worship song...
Take out your Bible and read slowly, thinking about what you read.
Write or draw any thoughts that come to mind in a prayer journal.
This is all best done in your own space alone with God.

Worship   **Bible**   **Prayer Journal**   **Quiet place**

TARGETED
Day 31

The wicked lie in wait for the righteous,
intent on putting them to death;

White trainers are "in" at the moment. They are super cool, but also retro as well. Who doesn't want to wear a pair of Nikes like Marty McFly from Back to the Future? Just think, they go well with anything, a dress, skirt, shorts, jeans, or cargo pants. However, there is one drawback from wearing white shoes, especially brand-new white shoes. Because they are super bright, those sneakers are going to attract all sorts of attention, some of it unwanted. You see, there's always someone who wants to step on them! Suddenly your beautiful clean look is now dirtied.

Unfortunately, much like those white shoes, the secret intent of the wicked towards the righteous is to make them appear no different from their own lives. "Why don't you swear?" they'll ask you, intent on making you do just that. They find it funny to provoke a reaction that causes you to get angry. "Why don't you look at these naked pictures?" they want to know, trying to lower your standards. They don't want you to be good, maybe because it shows up their evil deeds. Maybe the life you are living for God is making their consciences feel uneasy. They'll want you to blend in and be like

138

them. Let's be honest, it's a tough challenge to resist. Standing out makes you a target, whilst blending in is going to bring you less hassle.

We read today that some evil people are motivated to set a trap for those who follow God. They don't like the sense of innocence and purity that the faithful followers of Jesus carry. Do you ever feel that you are the target of such people? I know it's not nice, but it does mean you are doing something right! The enemy only attacks those he sees as a threat, those who are dangerous to his plans. He will use bullies and friends to isolate you into thinking you are strange in your desires to keep God's standards. One of the traps the enemy sets for us is to change the culture around us, highlighting us as a target to be attacked. What do I mean by "the culture around us"? It's basically what everybody else is doing, their belief system and how they act. Remember Daniel (Daniel chapter 6). King Darius instructed that a law be made for everyone to worship him for thirty days, forbidding prayer to God. Suddenly Daniel stood out when he continued to take time out to kneel before God in prayer. The enemy wants to cause us to compromise our beliefs, moral standards and actions, so that our witness for Jesus can be silenced. You may not be forced to worship a person, but there are certain beliefs and worldviews that many support today which directly contradict God's words. The pressure to agree with these and to actively support them is a growing threat to our witness to Jesus.

" This call to persevere and to hold fast to the testimony of Jesus, is not one we have to do alone. "

You'll probably not be surprised to hear that this is not a new thing. In the years after Jesus' death, it was the Roman Empire with its worship of many gods that challenged the faith of the followers of Jesus. In the culture of the day people were expected to declare that Caesar was Lord and burn incense in pagan temples. To many, this wasn't a problem, he was just another god among many; but for Christians there is only one God who can be worshipped (Exodus 20:1-3). Jesus' words to the people in such situations was to hold fast and remain faithful to Him (Revelation 3:10). This call to persevere and to hold fast to the testimony of Jesus, is not one we have to do alone. The Holy Spirit is given to help us to have the strength to endure trials and challenging times. He sees us when we take a stand for Him. Importantly, when you have held fast and not compromised your faith when pressured, it registers in heaven as having suffered for Jesus. Just as Jesus suffered for you and me, there are times of suffering that we go through for Him. The Bible tells us that by going through this and remaining faithful to Jesus, we are actually partnering in the sufferings that He went through for us (Philippians 3:10).

PRAY

Father God. Thank you for sending Your Son Jesus to cover all my wrong doing. I know that I am righteous because of You and not by my own good efforts. I need Your power to help me stand firm in the challenge.

Day 31

THE WICKED LIE IN WAIT
for the righteous,
INTENT ON PUTTING THEM
to death: but the lord will
NOT LEAVE THEM
in the power of
THE WICKED OR LET THEM BE
condemned when
BROUGHT TO TRIAL.

VINDICATED
Day 32

*but the L*ORD *will not leave them in the power of the wicked*
or let them be condemned when brought to trial.

Bullies. They just love to control other people. One tactic they use to achieve this is by false accusation. They'll accuse you of something you haven't done, or they will make up their own rules, which if you break, will make them feel justified in picking a fight with you. Just like Biff in the 'Back to the Future' films they'll say "I thought I told you not to come in here again." They restrict a person's freedom, using the fear of punishment to make you obey. Ever had this happen to you? It's likely that when treated like this, you'll feel powerless to do anything about it. This can be stressful and give us cause for worry.

The words we read today remind us of how God hates injustice. He understands injustice, not only because He sees it going on in the world, but also because He was on the receiving end of it when He was on earth. Jesus was totally innocent and yet according to the rule system of the religious leaders, they accused Him of being guilty. The execution Jesus endured was the worst imaginable. So, when it comes to you and me as His children, God is very concerned when we are treated unjustly.

Maybe you are currently experiencing a situation where you are feeling controlled or bullied, whether that is physically or mentally. Both ways can really wear you down and make you fret about what tomorrow holds. Jesus tells the story of a woman who is seeking justice and being denied it by a court judge who should know better. It's worth reading, because it gives us an insight into how to approach bullying situations and how God responds (see Luke 18:1-8). I used to think that the way to beat the power of a bully was either verbally or physically. This achieved both success and failure. Then one day I realised that in most cases my battles actually weren't going to be won with verbal excellence or physical ninja skills. Instead, my battles would be won through prayer beforehand. We read today that God's will is that the righteous do not remain under the power of the wicked. God works to see the innocent vindicated and for unfair treatment to end. When we pray according to this truth, we know that God will give us what we ask. So don't give up asking God for justice! Remember, we've already read in this Psalm that God uses their words and plans against them (see verses 14-15).

❝The words we read today remind us of how God hates injustice.❞

Therefore, rather than worrying what you are going to say or do, approach the situation in prayer. This doesn't mean telling God how He should fix the situation, instead pray for His help and guidance to navigate it all. God's promise is that those who persist in asking for justice will get that justice. If someone is bad mouthing you, God hears it and He knows the truth from the lies. As part of His acts of justice on your behalf, He will see to it that you will be vindicated and your reputation restored. It has to be said though that persistence is not generally a one-off activity! It indicates a time of ongoing prayer during the struggle before innocence is declared and evil is overcome. This requires patience from us, trusting God though we don't see what the outcome will be, even when things look bad. When our battles become God's battles, the bully's power over us will come to an end, of that there is no doubt!

How do we pray when we've been called to attend a meeting where false accusations are likely to surface? Ask for wisdom. God's gift of wisdom uses the truth to help you to deal with the tactics of the enemy. God will think of something that they won't have anticipated. They'll not know how to respond and their wrong motives will be exposed.

PRAY

Father God. I feel controlled by others and powerless to be able to do anything about it. Thank You that there is none more powerful than You. Thank you that You know exactly what is going on. Be my protector Lord. Please work behind the scenes to rescue me and give me the wisdom not to make the situation worse! In Jesus name!

Day 32

PRAYER SPACE

Maybe you're worried about a bullying situation? As children of God, Jesus doesn't want us to be fearful. He can do something about that. As a way of bringing them before God, you might like to write here some of the events that are making you feel fearful...

Take a look at Psalm 18 and begin to think around the words that you are reading that tell you about what God is like. Start to remind yourself that since God is with you, you will know all of the benefits that God brings. He wants to help you to see how He is working in your life. As you consider these things, draw a picture of yourself in the middle of the circle (it can be a stick person!).

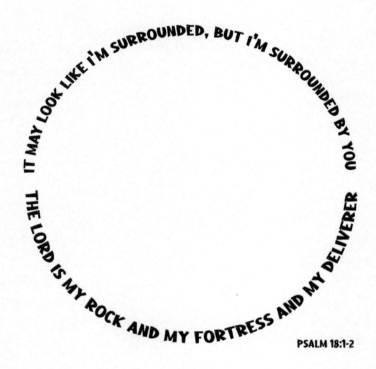

IT MAY LOOK LIKE I'M SURROUNDED, BUT I'M SURROUNDED BY YOU THE LORD IS MY ROCK AND MY FORTRESS AND MY DELIVERER

PSALM 18:1-2

INNER CONFIDENCE
Day 33

Hope in the LORD and keep his way.
He will exalt you to inherit the land;
when the wicked are destroyed, you will see it.

Would you wait for a bus if you didn't think it was running? What about that friend who promised to meet you after school, but has let you down before? The difficulty with such waiting is that we don't 100% know whether something is going to actually happen. This can happen when queuing online for tickets to see your favourite band or waiting for your grades on results day. The element of uncertainty about it can be unnerving. With all of these things there's an element of "I hope it'll be alright" (except for the exam results, where I'm sure you'll ace them!).

We're encouraged today to hope in the Lord. The meaning behind this word hope brings together two ideas: waiting and confidence. Say you've been talking to God about some issues going on in your life and they haven't been resolved. It's not that God is going to do nothing about it, but rather you're in that place called waiting. Not everything happens immediately. When we're waiting for God to bring our solution, it can appear that there's a delay to our plans being fulfilled. However, from God's perspective it's just the process being worked out. So when we're encouraged to hope in the Lord, it's not a case of "Just hope it'll be alright." Instead, it can be described as a confidence that God is in charge, therefore things will turn out well. He is working on our behalf.

To hope in the Lord is to confidently wait for God in your struggles. Involve God in every part of the situation, no matter how well or badly things seem to be going. Thank Him for each and every blessing whether large or small, rather than fretting about how things are not as they should be. Sometimes we can even give our fears more credit that they are actually due. Give God the credit He is due. Put your full confidence in Him.

It's easy to think "I will stop worrying when ... happens." When I've finished my exams, or when this or that situation is resolved. Yet God actually wants us to have joy in the journey. It's not just the joy of having achieved an A star. God wants you and me to find His peace and joy during the challenge and in the struggles we are facing. This is everyday life and not just the end result. The problem when worry is always focused on the big event, is that when that event is over and that target achieved, there is always another one on the horizon.

"To hope in the Lord is to confidently wait for God in your struggles."

You and I need to learn the art of letting go of worry and enjoying the challenge. Put your hope in the positive plans that the Lord has for you, rather than any negative scenarios that a soon to be destroyed enemy might have up his sleeve. Rather than fearing the worst, why not remember what the Apostle Paul said "I can do all things through Christ who gives me strength" (Philippians 4:13). Don't hold off

148

receiving the Lord's joy until tomorrow. Rather than dreading what's coming up, "Hope in the Lord and Keep his way," for He will exalt you with His strength where you are weak.

Hope is a confidence in the goodness of God. It's a trust in His good character, knowing that He will act according to His words and His promises. When we become followers of Jesus, we change our attitude from one of doubt to faith, having become fully confident of our future. This brings peace to the heart and strength to the soul, which makes us more ready to take on the challenges of today and tomorrow.

PRAY

Father God. Today I choose to put my confidence in You. I give to you my fears of things that have not yet happened. Thank You that You are good and that Your love for me endures forever. Thank You for the good things that You did for me yesterday. I know that You are working on my behalf. I can face today, being enabled by Your power. Change my doubting ways! In Jesus' name!

Day 33

THINGS I AM IN AWE OF

THINGS YOU ARE BRILLIANT AT GOD

SONGS I WANT TO SING TO YOU

LITTLE ROOTS
Day 34

I have seen a wicked and ruthless man
flourishing like a luxuriant native tree,[36] but he soon passed away
and was no more; though I looked for him, he could not be found.

Ever had your parents tell you that things were much tougher at school "back in their day"? Maybe they've told you how they had a ten-mile hike to the bus stop every day, or they had to do physical education barefoot in sub zero temperatures? Well, I once walked to school during a hurricane! It was October 1987 and I lived in London. It was a bit breezy outside, but you can really only see the power of the wind by looking at the movement of the trees. We thought it was safe to go out, because during the lunchtime weather report the previous day, Michael Fish the weather man had said:

"Earlier on today, apparently a woman rang the BBC and said she heard there was a hurricane on the way. Well, if you're watching, there isn't... it will become very windy, mostly in Spain and France."

Hours later, the UK was hit by the most severe storm for three hundred years, causing fifteen million trees to fall. The damage was estimated in the region of £1.5 billion (which was a lot in those days). With trees blocking train tracks, roads and even falling on houses, all that could be done was to saw them up and have them removed. When I finally got to school, I was promptly sent home, back into the hurricane! Who would have predicted it? Not the weather people!

We read today, about a man, a bully, appearing to be as strong as a well-established tree that has become part of the landscape. The idea comes from the famous cedar trees of Lebanon, strong, powerful and successful. If you were to point to such a tree and tell your friend, "This time tomorrow the wind will blow and that tree will have fallen down," they would laugh at you. Impossible! Much like the Psalmist, we can observe the apparent success of the wicked and consider them unstoppable. They have influence and use their power to control and oppress others. How could things be any different we wonder? Yet, although this "wicked and ruthless man" may have the appearance of success, it turns out that his roots have no depth. That is where he is vulnerable. He's not as strong as he makes out. At any time he could fall, toppled more easily than anyone thought possible.

Here, we're encouraged to see things from God's perspective instead of our own. To focus on a bully in his or her success is to give them power over us; but we're told here that their success is only temporary. All is not as it appears. The wicked do not have the power over their own destiny. They are not in charge. Their roots are not secured in God, therefore they are like a house built on sand. God is on the throne. He is the Lord of hosts. The God who brings justice for the innocent who cry out to Him, will send a storm that makes easy work of such people. At which point they have the chance to turn from their wicked ways or be toppled.

"Here, we're encouraged to see things from God's perspective instead of our own.**"**

Consider this for a moment; imagine that person who has been giving you grief day in day out, is no longer in your life. You get up in the morning and they're not on your mind. You're going into school without having to think of the battles you'll have to face, of the struggle just to focus on what you're there to do. Instead, you're making your way home thinking about football, Minecraft, dance moves or whatever. The bully is out of your life, out of your thinking, they're no longer a concern. God wants you to experience this freedom. He even wants you to feel like this now, in the middle of your troubles. God's encouragement to you today is: entrust your day to Him. He is with you. He is working on your behalf. Don't let your thinking enlarge the power of the bully. He or she is a tree with little roots. Their time will come and they'll be gone from your life for good.

PRAY

Father God. You know me. You know my thoughts. Please give my mind peace from the effects of the bully. Make my heart stronger. In Jesus' name.

Day 34

DEEP ROOTS
Day 35

Consider the blameless, observe the upright;
a future awaits those who seek peace.

If you've ever seen a Marvel film, you'd have most likely come across the character Thor. He's one of the most powerful Avengers; but there's a moment in one film where he discovers his powers are limited. His weapon of choice, a hammer that gives him the ability to wield lightning, becomes unbearably heavy when Thor's bad attitude makes him unworthy of using it. No matter what strength he has, the hammer remains immovable. Only when Thor's attitude changes, does he become worthy of using the hammer.

In the verse we read today, we're encouraged to consider those who are humble and selfless. Unlike fictional characters, or those who fake it, the blameless are worthy people, whose good attitudes come from following God. It's probably easier to honour God and His ways when faced with little to challenge a person's moral actions. However, the test comes when the tough circumstances emerge. A person can appear blameless when everyone around them is on their side, but what happens when things are not going their way? The ruthless will likely resort to lies and deception when it suits their

155

cause. The blameless are those who refuse to bend the truth, even when a difficult situation is easier solved that way. Although their self-sacrifice may go unnoticed, the truth is more important to them than using lies or manipulation to keep up appearances.

This verse has a link to the one we read yesterday. We're given another contrast to consider: an aggressive man who appears as strong as a tree, who has no future, with a humble person who will outlast the wicked, because he or she wants peace. Here, it's all about the depth of our roots. Do you ever stop to think of what is true, right, pure, lovely, admirable, excellent or praiseworthy?[4] What we let into our minds will determine the attitudes of our hearts. Just like the way the words and actions of social media influencers can shape the hobbies or spending habits of followers, so our thoughts influence who we are. What are those things that your mind dwells on? Are they rooted in God?

> **"The blameless are those who refuse to bend the truth, even when a difficult situation is easier solved that way."**

When a person gives their life to follow Jesus, the Holy Spirit becomes your influencer. He will inspire your thoughts with the good things of God. When our roots are drawing on the true, pure and lovely things of God we'll behave differently. Friendship with God is the place where righteousness blossoms; because the closer we are to God, the more we'll discover about Him and become like Him. As God works in us, transforming our minds and renewing us in our spirit, a passion begins to burn inside to please God with our life. The shallow acts of the wicked fail, because their selfish ways lead to destruction; but the blameless have their roots deeply set in God.

156

A humble person knows they're not perfect. To be righteous in God's book is to believe in His Son Jesus. When we turn from our wrong and selfish ways to do things His way, Jesus' sacrifice makes us blameless. It's God who has made the way possible for us to have peace with Him, through faith in Jesus. When we begin to notice God's goodness in our lives, it's tempting to think this is something we've achieved. Although it is a partnership with God, our blameless status is always only because of Jesus' sacrifice for us and not because of our own good deeds. It's God's power working in us that leads us to live blameless lives. God has a future prepared for all who come to Him in this way, which starts on earth and continues forever into the afterlife.

PRAY

Holy Spirit of the Living God. I want You to be my influencer. Help me to see when I'm being selfish or using deceptive ways. I know that these have nothing to do with the way You work. Please influence me. Show me more of Jesus and the Father. Help me to understand the words of the Bible. I want You to transform my life that I may follow Jesus with all my heart. In Jesus' name.

Day 35

PRAYER SPACE

These are lyrics from a song that originated from the writings of a Chinese Christian named Watchman Nee.

Let me love without honour.
Let me serve without applause.
Let me suffer, no-one knowing,
Live for Jesus without praise.

Let me walk without turning,
Follow you mocked and betrayed,
Pressing forward, hold the vision,
Many pressures, no complaints.

Just poured-out wine,
Just broken bread;
My life poured out others to bless.
Shed blood and tears and suffer loss,
And win the crown and love the cross.

Let me grieve without comfort,
Give up ease, pay any price.
I will live in Your completeness;
Fruitful in love's sacrifice.

Let me live true to Zion;
Covenant! Never betray!
Separated, faithful, eager -
I will tread the highest way!

Let others be drawn to me, Lord,
And find in me Your precious wounds.
My life I give as drink and food
Just poured-out wine, just broken bread.

How do these words describe what living for Jesus
is all about?

Do these words highlight any attitudes that need to
change in your own heart?

CALLED TO ACCOUNT
Day 36

But all sinners will be destroyed;
there will be no future for the wicked.

Years ago, I bought a car from a car dealer. It was beautiful. Taking up all of our savings, it was a spacious vehicle with a glass roof, electric everything, and a red metallic finish. A dream to drive. Unfortunately, not long after buying it, the car had a loss of power which was accompanied by smoke pouring out of the back and filling the inside of the car. We all got out of the car knowing it was probably done. I returned the car to the dealer in the hope of having it fixed, since it was within the warranty. How long would it take to fix? Only a couple of weeks I was told.

Unfortunately, when a couple of weeks were over, it wasn't ready. Just another week the dealer said... and another week. A week turned into a month, which turned into a whole year. I rang them, but no reply. Was I now being ghosted? So I went down to the car dealership to check on progress, but everything was gone. No cars, no office, no people. They had cleared out. There I was, with no car, no money and no dealership to go back to. I felt cheated, lied to and angry. Oh, the injustice!! However, in my conversations with Jesus, He was reassuring me that this was not the end.

How could I get my money back if I didn't know how to contact the dealer? After giving up for a while, I felt inspired to try looking up the sales guy on social media. My search was a success! He'd opened another car dealership about ten miles away. "Oh, we are nothing to do with that other dealership" I was told. So things turned legal. After a process that took another year, I finally secured a court judgement against the dealership owner's house. Now he couldn't sell his home without giving me my money! That week I had a phone call. The dealer wanted to send me the money that I had paid for the car! I was so thankful to God who had given me justice at last!

Why do you think God gave Moses the Ten Commandments? Some people think that the laws God gave us are to spoil their fun. However, if you've ever been on the receiving end of lies or theft, you'll know that it isn't fun. Today, we're told that justice will one day catch up with the wicked. These are people who have chosen to live in rebellion to God and his ways. What is a sinner? It's someone who does wrong against other people and against God. It's a selfishness that has made up its own rules; something we are all guilty of. God has made us aware of this moral standard not to kill our joy, but that we might live in peace with each other.

Here, we're reassured that God will take responsibility for dealing with those intent on injustice against the innocent. It's tempting to take the law into our own hands and do the same things that the wicked do, to get our own back. However, if we resort to evil ways, we're taking away God's opportunity to handle it (see Romans 12:19). During our time of struggle, we often wonder what's the future of the wicked? When will they see the justice they deserve? We're promised in these verses that the innocent have a future, which in contrast the wicked don't. The difference between the righteous and the wicked is that the righteous are living in a state of blessing and the wicked one of disaster. So let God handle it, by obeying His ways. In every step of the struggle, keep going back to Jesus to discover what to do next.

> ❝ If we resort to evil ways, we're taking away God's opportunity to handle it. ❞

In the struggle against injustice, it's easy to be taken in by the apparent success of those who do evil. Just because they appear to be getting away with it, doesn't mean that they'll escape a future of divine judgement. God's promise to you is that such people will be called to account for their actions.

PRAY

Father God. I love Your ways. You are totally good, pure and holy. I commit to follow Your ways. I surrender my desire to make my own way. I realise that You actually want me to depend on You. Help me to trust You in everything I do, as I go through my struggle for justice. In Jesus' name!

Day 36

JOURNAL SPACE

but all sinners will be destroyed; there

WILL BE NO FUTURE FOR THE WICKED.

אָלֶפְבֵּ'ת

DO YOU BELIEVE IT??
Day 37

The salvation of the righteous comes from the LORD;

Do you ever get a song stuck in your head that you just can't forget? It's there when you're walking down the road (baby shark, do do do), when you're eating your lunch (mummy shark, do do do) and when you're trying to get to sleep (grandma shark do do do). It could be a popular melody, catchy words or just repetitive, but it's there stuck on repeat, unforgettable.

Since we're nearing the end of Psalm 37, I think it's time to let you into a little secret about this one. Originally written as a song, each verse would have begun with a different letter of the Hebrew alphabet. Maybe you had to do an acrostic poem in Junior High School where you have one word written vertically, with horizontal sentences beginning with each letter of that word.

What's the significance of each verse starting with a different letter of the alphabet? The answer is to aid the memory. The whole thing is written so that we'll remember it. You may have come across words, phrases and ideas that appear to repeat. One way to remember something is to read or repeat it three times. Somehow the third time you do it, the thought starts to sink into the brain. Just like you may have learned your alphabet by being taught a song to learn, here the intention is that important spiritual principles would be retained. In ancient times followers of God didn't have Bibles to take home with them. They would go to their local temple when parts of the Scriptures would be read out.

This leads us to ask a very important question. What's the main takeaway from the whole Psalm? We've looked at the detail. What is God saying to you and me through each verse? Throughout this Psalm we are being taught to trust that God will rescue us. We've just read today, "The salvation of the righteous comes from the Lord." This is a thought that repeats throughout the Psalm, with the instruction "Do not fret." The reason why? It's because God is one of justice who rescues those who are His.

You might be wondering, "Why would the followers of God be tempted to doubt this truth about Him?" It's because it is possible to think that God has left us when things are going against us and we're suffering at the hands of the wicked. But fretting leads to all kinds of unnecessary negative stuff that will do us no good. The words that we've been reading don't deny that we'll have tough times. Sometimes such difficulties will take time to work through, requiring our patience and continued trust in God. Why would God's word be talking about Him saving us from trouble if everything was always peachy?

> **❝ Throughout this Psalm we are being taught to trust that God will rescue us. ❞**

There will be times when our faith in God and his ability to help us is tested. Often this is where genuine faith in Him is proved true. When life does not always go as we hope or plan, how we respond is important. God doesn't want us to forget that we can always find help in Him. Will you trust in God's solution when it seems impossible? He's our place of safety in the middle of the challenges that life throws at us. He's the one who will bring us through our troubles and out to the other side. Remember that He has an inheritance for us, both now and in the life to come. We're not only rescued from something bad, we're also rescued to something good. Jesus has good things in store for your future! I know that the thought of difficulties ahead is not a nice one, but as someone who has been through their fair share, King David reminds us that God does not fail to rescue those who trust in Him. David, the guy who had to face up to the most famous bully ever known (Goliath), reminds us that God is faithful to those who love Him. We have a good future to look forward to, because of the loving kindness of our God. Don't forget it!

PRAY

Father God. Thank You that You have good things in store for me. I know that Your plans cannot be stopped. I'm going to trust in You. In Jesus' name.

Day 37

Jesus. What do you love about me?

What Bible verses are you bringing to my mind?

Holy Spirit. Please show me more of what Jesus is like.

Father God. What are your dreams for my life?

SHIELDED
Day 38

*The salvation of the righteous comes from the LORD;
he is their stronghold in time of trouble.*

Imagine you're a king, back in Medieval times and you live on an island the size of the United Kingdom. You're surrounded by other nations, but divided by water. How would you defend yourself against the threat of potential invaders? The answer? Castles. This is exactly what the Tudor King, Henry VIII did. King Henry set about a project to establish coastal forts, to make land attacks a tricky proposition. If you were to launch an offensive on Deal castle in Kent, you would discover that it has two hundred ports available to fire artillery at you. With a series of castles along the coast, Henry was able to establish his kingdom, putting off others who might try to take it from him.

The advantage of such a strategy was that there was no doubt where King Henry's kingdom was. These castles stood for the strength and presence of his kingdom in the land. This image of God as our stronghold tells us that we are a part of His kingdom and that He is our place of refuge, shielding us from attack. We are His. God is our strong defence against the enemy. If life is becoming overwhelming, God is the one we can be secure in and run to for peace, protection and safety. Like an impenetrable fortress, God stands in the way of the enemy's attacks and says "You shall not pass!"

Much like King Henry's strongholds, if an enemy were to attempt a beach landing, those who attacked were actually the ones at most risk. They were at a disadvantage and would be the ones to suffer loss from heavy artillery that would sink oncoming ships. Such forts were well equipped with an army, ready to fend off invaders. Attackers would very much regret ever attempting to overcome such a kingdom. God is an even greater stronghold. Not only are you His to look after, He will come to your defence with an attack against the enemy. God will make those who target His faithful ones regret ever starting anything! They'll find troubles of their own coming their way. Remember, He's the King of angel armies!

Having given God your life, you are His. No enemy can snatch you out of His hand.[5] God will protect you because you are His possession. You are a son or a daughter in His house, part of His family and His kingdom. This gives you access to God and His armoury against the attacks of the enemy (to find out more, check out the next page).

66 God will make those who target His faithful ones regret ever starting anything! 99

You see, some difficulties that we face have a spiritual force behind them. If someone takes a disliking to you, it could just be that that person is just acting out of natural idiotic ignorance. However, it's important to also recognise that there are times when another power is at work behind the scenes. One strategy of our enemy, the devil, is to use his forces to influence others to have bad feeling against

God's people. There will be times when we experience conflict that has nothing to do with our own actions, but because we are faithfully following Jesus. Thankfully, we have God to run to as our refuge. Delighting in Him will certainly help your soul to be at peace and you may gain insight into God's perspective on all that is going on. Prayer is a powerful weapon, leading to heaven's armoury. Your faith will be strengthened and you'll witness God doing amazing things, bringing about a success in your life that will make the enemy regret he ever tried to harm you.

PRAY

Father God. Thank You that You are my fortress and my stronghold. Because of Your loving kindness, I know that I am safe with You. I come to this place of prayer glad that I can connect with You. You are the true, real and Living God, the Lord of angel armies, the Almighty. There is none as strong as You, or as loving and kind. I worship You, my Saviour and my King! Jesus I love You!

Day 38

PRAYER SPACE

You'll need to read Ephesians 6:10-18!

The belt of truth

This is to read and understand God's words, so that each day you will be prepared in your heart with God's perspective if fear comes knocking.

What recurring fears are bothering you?

Ask God to show you what is not true about these fears.

Ask God to give you a truth about what He is like.

The breastplate of righteousness

Having thought about God's words, ask Him how to put this truth into action (truth followed brings protection). Live it out and make it part of your life. This will protect your heart.

What truth are you going to remember when you are attacked by negative fears?

Feet fitted in readiness/Gospel of peace

Take God with you wherever you go and release God's favour on others so that others will understand and discover Jesus too.

Is there someone you know who is going through something similar?

What can you do to help them through it?

The shield of faith

Keep a barrier between you and those negative words. Reject the lies that come to mind by replacing them with God's truth about who you really are. Believe these words are true and trust Him for all you need. This will protect you from random attacks.

What do you need God to provide for you today?

Instead of worrying, let it go in your mind and depend on Him to help you with the things you can't do.

Helmet of Salvation

Having believed and received Jesus as friend and King of your life, live out your relationship with Jesus by connecting regularly with Him in conversation. This will protect your mind.

Invite Jesus into your day, or whatever you are currently doing. Welcome His presence with you as you go through your day. Renew your mind with His words everyday

The sword of the Spirit

Speak out the words of the Lord as He inspires you. Take those times to praise Him from the evidence you have discovered in His word. This will enable you to destroy the works that the devil is trying to establish in you.

What truth have you read from the Bible today? Speak it out over your difficulties and trust that God will deliver you from them all.

WHOSE SIDE ARE YOU ON?
Day 39

The salvation of the righteous comes from the LORD; he is their stronghold in time of trouble. [40]The LORD helps them and delivers them; he delivers them from the wicked and saves them, because they take refuge in him.

It was June 22nd 1986, I was twelve years old. England had made it through to the quarter-finals of football's World Cup. We were playing Argentina. Our line-up of players was strong, demonstrating in previous games that they could play well as a team. With Gary Lineker as our striker, there was every hope that we could actually win the game. Argentina had great players too, with one Diego Maradona dubbed the best player in the world.

With no goals in the first half, hopes were high that we could nick a goal and win it. But then it happened, one of the most unjust moments of sporting history. After some pressure from the Argentines, England tried to clear the ball from the England penalty box. A miss kick sent the ball looping up into the air towards our own goal. Maradona was positioned, jumping to head the ball into the England net. In the ball went, leaving the referee to declare 1-0 to Argentina. However, something looked very suspicious. Maradona appeared to use his hand and not his head, knocking it over

England's goalie Peter Shilton!! As players protested to the ref, Maradona celebrated as if he had scored a fair goal.

In those days there was no VAR technology for the ref to replay the goal. As we watched our television screens, replays clearly showed Maradona deliberately using his hand to score the goal. The only help the referee had at the time was his own eyes, those of the nearest linesmen and the honesty of those playing. In interviews after the game Maradona was famously quoted as saying that he scored "A little with the head of Maradona and a little with the hand of God."

Have you noticed sometimes how the words of some people don't match up with their actions? Even some celebrities tell of their faith in God in award speeches, but when you take a look at their lives, it doesn't take much to wonder whose side they are actually on. Can you really be on God's side if you deliberately break the ninth commandment (do not lie) in a high-profile sporting event? Of course, we all make mistakes, yet if the actions of our lives demonstrate that we are living in rebellion to God's ways, we might find we're on the wrong side of God. Instead of being counted as His, we've turned to our own way.

The moment that we come to Jesus, it's the beginning of a new life, where we surrender our wants to His will and turn from the wrong actions that we used to do. Rather than being a one-off decision, choosing to follow Jesus is a lifestyle, continually choosing His way for our lives. In the bit we read, we see two distinct sides. One way leads to life and the other toward conflict with God. Can we expect to be saved by God when we've chosen a way which rejects his reign over the things that we do? Although it isn't our good deeds that will save us, our faithfulness to the Lord is seen in what we do. What we do comes from what we believe. Therefore, if our actions are telling us that we are not following God, we need to do something about it before it's too late.

> **"** Can we expect to be saved by God when we've chosen a way which rejects his reign over the things that we do? **"**

If this is the case for you, it's time to choose who you want to be the king of your life. Are there parts of your life where you're still in charge? Is it the language that you use? Or the things you often talk about? Maybe it's your conversations and enjoying a good gossip, perpetuating lies about others? We can't cheat God like Maradona cheated the world. For God to be our place of safety, we need to submit the whole of our lives to His Lordship.

PRAY

Father God. I know that you want all of my heart and not just a part of it. I want you to be my shelter and my Saviour. I'm sorry for times I have chosen my own way, knowing it was contrary to your ways. For You to be the first in my heart, I know I have to change my ways. Jesus I love You!

Day 39

176

PRAYER SPACE

The Bible tells us that God so loved the world (that is us), that He gave His only Son that whoever believes in Him shall not perish but have everlasting life (John 3:16).

Q - Do you believe that God came to earth for you?
Q - Do you believe that Jesus lived and died for you?
Q - Do you believe that God loves you?

The Bible says that no one is perfect; that we have all done wrong and fallen short of God's standard. Heaven is a perfect place where God is, but we being imperfect are separated from God without Jesus.

Q - Do you admit that you have done wrong?
Q - Are you sorry for those things you have done?
Q - Would you like God to forgive you?

The Bible contains eye witness accounts of how the Romans executed Jesus through the torture of nailing Him to a cross (John 19). God purposed this to happen so that ours wrongs could be erased. He rose from the dead three days later demonstrating that He was God's Son (see John 20).

Q – Do you believe Jesus was God's only Son?
Q – Do you believe that He died for you?
Q – Do you believe He rose from the dead?

Jesus said "Whoever wants to become my disciple must deny themselves and take up their cross and follow me." (Matthew 16:24).

Q – Will you receive God's free gift of wrongs forgiven and eternal life with Him in heaven?
Q – Do you choose to live your life for Jesus?

PRAYER SPACE

Whether you've been to church loads of times or never set foot inside a church, God wants you to know Him. When you pray this prayer, something will happen. God will come close to you whether you sense Him close or not. He wants you to know that you are His forever!

If you have chosen to follow Jesus, please pray this prayer...

> *Dear Lord God; Almighty God, I come to You as a stranger, but I want to be Your friend.*
>
> *I know that in Your deep love for me You welcome me. Thank You for sending Jesus into the world to show me what You are like. I believe He is Your Son and that He lived on this earth and that He was executed by the Romans. Thank You that You planned this in order that I could be made free; free from the power of the enemy over my life and free to be forgiven for all of my wrongs.*
>
> *I believe Jesus rose from the dead and that I can know Him with me every day.*
>
> *Please forgive me for all the wrong things that I have done. I am truly sorry. In respect for You, I turn away from the wrong things I have done and choose to follow You. Help me to live my life for You.*
>
> *Now I ask You to come and take over my heart and my life.*
> *In Jesus' name!*

Once you have taken this step with God, the Bible calls you a child of God *"Yet to all who did receive Him, to those who believed in His name, He gave the right to become children of God"* (John 1:12). This means that you have peace with God; and God as the best loving Father includes you in His family and will guide you in life, protect you and provide for the things you need. This is the start of a wonderful friendship with God!

MAKING IT THROUGH
Day 40

If you've ever seen the reality TV Show *The Apprentice*, you'll know it's all about business start-up wannabees and their attempts to make money through a series of weekly tasks. At the end of each week's challenge, candidates are fired for giving the worst contribution to the task. When there are only four candidates left, they enter the *scary* interview stage. Here, interviewees are grilled by four top executives, who go through every detail of the entrant's applications, looking for errors, lies and any exaggerations. One particular interviewer, Claude Littner is well-known for his gruff manner and no-nonsense approach. After going through the details of one person's business plan, he famously concluded "You don't know how much you don't know, because you don't know!" I'm sure this is something no one wants to hear at their job interview, but when they are asking for £250,000 to run their business, it could save a person from making a huge mistake!

Think about this for a minute. The future is uncertain. We don't even know what we are going to face tomorrow. There are many things about our day that we *can* expect and influence, but there are also many things we cannot predict or control. In this Psalm we're given the thoughts of a wise man who has experienced a life lived hand-in-hand with God. Contained within this Psalm is the way to make it through it all.

So don't fret. Burning with anger leads to hot-headed responses which just make things worse. Also don't become preoccupied or fixated on that person who you think is going to ruin your life. Worrying about their potential influence over your life, is giving them more power than they actually have or deserve. To do this is to actually mistrust the power and rule which God has over the entire universe! Don't assume that the worst is going to happen, because you just don't know that!

Instead of getting wound up and anxious about what the ungodly are doing, take time to be still before God. There's a lot said about mindfulness these days and doing things to keep your mind healthy. The busyness of life and the distraction of mobile devices can overload the brain. Therefore, take time to be still with Jesus. If it helps, use the prayer spaces to guide your time with God with an open Bible. They are there to help you connect with Jesus in a real way, so that you can leave that place feeling refreshed and renewed by His power.

To live our lives in fear of what we don't know, will only make us miserable. God wants His people to win! He has plans for you to succeed. He has an inheritance to pass on to you. The inexperienced person doesn't know stuff. What we have read in this Psalm are the thoughts of an old man, an experienced follower of God who does know! These words are also from the Lord. They are like good fruit to be eaten, that will do your heart good when you take them to heart and fully trust what God is saying.

But what about the current trials that you are going through? Tough times, bullies, school pressures, difficult relationships or other challenges can make it difficult to see the ways in which God is working for our good. The Lord is with you through it all, helping you to persevere. Success is not all about exams, sports trophies or YouTube subscribers. Making it through the toughest of times is a success in itself. If that is where you are at and you are enduring hardship, you are a champion! So keep going, don't give up!

❝ To live our lives in fear of what we don't know, will only make us miserable. ❞

Don't forget, God's way is the way of justice. He is working to prevent the schemes of the ungodly and give the actions of the wicked what they justly deserve. You and I don't know what God is up to; but where He asks us to trust Him, we know that He is up to something good!

Father God. I don't know what tomorrow will bring, but I do know that You were with me yesterday, You're with me now and You're waiting for me in my tomorrows. Thank You that You love me. I love You too! In Jesus' name!

PRAYER SPACE

If you would like to take God up on His invitation to know Him, you can do this by praying this prayer to Him. If you can speak (or whisper) it, all the better!

Thank You Jesus for Your invitation.

I come just as I am.

I know I have done many things wrong.

I thank You for dying on the cross for me.

Cleanse my life.

Set me free from the past.

I open the door of my life now.

I receive Your invitation.

I receive You into my life.

Come in by Your Holy Spirit.

Fill me with Your peace, Your presence, Your power.

Help me to build my life on You

Thank You Jesus for hearing my prayer.

You are now a follower of Jesus and part of God's family!!! Why not draw, write, doodle or scribble down anything that you want to say to God...

END NOTES

1.   "Ducky" Dr Mallard NCIS Season 14 Episode 13

2.   If someone is causing you harm, this is a serious crime and should always be dealt with. If you aren't ready to contact the Police, there are organisations you can contact with people who know what to do if you feel threatened or in danger. These are free private and confidential services where children and young people can talk about anything.

Here are some UK based organisations who have dedicated staff who can help you:
Childline – www.childline.org.uk – 0800 1111
NSPCC – www.nspcc.org.uk - 0808 800 5000 (For adults concerned about a child).
Runaway helpline – www.runawahelpline.org.uk – 116 000
Samaritans – 116 123

Those based in the USA can call:
Childhelp – www.childhelphotline.org – 1-800-422-4453
Runaway safe line - www.1800runaway.org/youth-teens - 1-800-786-2929
Crisis text - www.crisistextline.org – Text HOME to 741741 (to connect with a counsellor)

Those who live in Canada can call:
Kids help phone – www.kidshelpphone.ca – 1 800 668-6868
Fondation Tel Jeunes - www.fondationteljeunes.org – 1 800 361-5085

3.   Pile S. (1979) The book of Heroic Failures, Penguin Books Ltd, 1979. (P. 86).

4.   Philippians 4:8 - Check it out, it's awesome.

5.   John 10:29

To help you with your regular Bible study,
why not try these out...

DEVOTIONS WITH A DIFFERENCE!

| A recipe for faith | Finding identity | Unlocking Revelation |
| Psalm 37 | Psalm 139 | Revelation |

Inspire.
DEVOTIONS AND RESOURCES

Visit our website:
www.inspiredevotions.com

Resources

Home   Devotions   Youth Ministry Resources   Journalling   Youth Games   Shop   Blog   The Author   Contact Us

Inspire.

RESOURCES AND DEVOTIONS FOR BUSY PEOPLE

Blog

Games ideas

Amy Walters

Christian Graphic Design Artist
Logos, Print Design, Social Media Design

https://www.bloom-creative.co.uk/
hello@bloom-creative.co.uk

Printed in Great Britain
by Amazon

34265332R00104